1 Corinthians: A Community in Dissent

T&T CLARK STUDY GUIDES TO THE NEW TESTAMENT

Series Editor:

Tat-siong Benny Liew, College of the Holy Cross, USA

Other titles in the series include:

1, 2, 3 John: An Introduction and Study Guide
1 & 2 Thessalonians: An Introduction and Study Guide
1 Peter: An Introduction and Study Guide
2 Corinthians: An Introduction and Study Guide
Colossians: An Introduction and Study Guide
Ephesians: An Introduction and Study Guide
Galatians: An Introduction and Study Guide
Hebrews: An Introduction and Study Guide
James: An Introduction and Study Guide
John: An Introduction and Study Guide
Luke: An Introduction and Study Guide
Mark: An Introduction and Study Guide
Matthew: An Introduction and Study Guide
Philemon: An Introduction and Study Guide
Philippians: An Introduction and Study Guide
Revelation: An Introduction and Study Guide
Romans: An Introduction and Study Guide
The Acts of the Apostles: An Introduction and Study Guide

T&T CLARK STUDY GUIDES TO THE OLD TESTAMENT

Exodus: An Introduction and Study Guide
Jonah, Micah and Nahum: An Introduction and Study Guide
Amos: An Introduction and Study Guide
1 & 2 Chronicles: An Introduction and Study Guide

1 & 2 Kings: An Introduction and Study Guide

1 & 2 Samuel: An Introduction and Study Guide

Daniel: An Introduction and Study Guide

Ecclesiastes: An Introduction and Study Guide

Exodus: An Introduction and Study Guide

Ezra-Nehemiah: An Introduction and Study Guide

Genesis: An Introduction and Study Guide

Haggai, Zechariah and Malachi: An Introduction and Study Guide

Isaiah: An Introduction and Study Guide

Jeremiah: An Introduction and Study Guide

Job: An Introduction and Study Guide

Joel, Obadiah, Habakkuk, Zephaniah: An Introduction and Study Guide

Joshua: An Introduction and Study Guide

Lamentations: An Introduction and Study Guide

Leviticus: An Introduction and Study Guide

Numbers: An Introduction and Study Guide

Proverbs: And Introduction and Study Guide

Psalms: An Introduction and Study Guide

Song of Songs: An Introduction and Study Guide

1 Corinthians: A Community in Dissent

An Introduction and Study Guide

Ekaputra Tupamahu

t&tclark
LONDON · NEW YORK · OXFORD · NEW DELHI · SYDNEY

T&T CLARK
Bloomsbury Publishing Plc, 50 Bedford Square, London, WC1B 3DP, UK
Bloomsbury Publishing Inc, 1359 Broadway, New York, NY 10018, USA
Bloomsbury Publishing Ireland, 29 Earlsfort Terrace, Dublin 2, D02 AY28, Ireland

BLOOMSBURY, T&T CLARK and the T&T Clark logo are trademarks of
Bloomsbury Publishing Plc

First published in Great Britain 2026

Copyright © Ekaputra Tupamahu, 2026

Ekaputra Tupamahu has asserted his right under the Copyright,
Designs and Patents Act, 1988, to be identified as Author of this work.

Cover design: clareturner.co.uk

All rights reserved. No part of this publication may be: i) reproduced or transmitted in
any form, electronic or mechanical, including photocopying, recording or by means of
any information storage or retrieval system without prior permission in writing from
the publishers; or ii) used or reproduced in any way for the training, development or
operation of artificial intelligence (AI) technologies, including generative AI technologies.
The rights holders expressly reserve this publication from the text and data mining
exception as per Article 4(3) of the Digital Single Market Directive (EU) 2019/790.

Bloomsbury Publishing Plc does not have any control over, or responsibility for, any
third-party websites referred to or in this book. All internet addresses given in this book
were correct at the time of going to press. The author and publisher regret
any inconvenience caused if addresses have changed or sites have ceased to exist,
but can accept no responsibility for any such changes.

A catalogue record for this book is available from the British Library.

A catalog record for this book is available from the Library of Congress.

ISBN:	HB:	978-0-5676-9354-9
	PB:	978-0-5676-7691-7
	ePDF:	978-0-5676-7692-4
	eBook:	978-0-5676-7693-1

Series: T&T Clark's Study Guides to the New Testament

Typeset by Integra Software Services Pvt. Ltd.
Printed and bound in Great Britain

For product safety related questions contact productsafety@bloomsbury.com.

To find out more about our authors and books visit www.bloomsbury.com
and sign up for our newsletters.

To Jeanny Grace Trifen Rumuat
I am forever grateful for your unwavering love and companionship.

CONTENTS

Introduction 1
    The Author's Intention? 2
    The Corinthian "Slogans" 4
    Re-presentation 6
    Sympathetic Reading 8
    The Plan of the Book 9

1 Paul's Correspondence with the Corinthians 13
    An Ancient Letter 13
    The Correspondence 16
    The Structure of 1 Corinthians 18
    In Closing 21

2 Guiding the Way: An Overview of the Letter and the City 23
    An Overview of the Contents of 1 Corinthians 23
        The Opening Section 23
        Response to an Indirect Source 24
        Response to a Direct Source 25
        The Closing Section 29
    The City of Corinth 29
        A Destroyed and Colonized City 30
        The Corinthians 32
    In Closing 34

3 Paul and the Corinthian Defiance 35
    The Description of Acts 35
    The Description of 1 Corinthians 39
        Are the Corinthians Really Divided? 40
        Paul's Concern: Authority, Not Division 42
        Paul and Apollos 43
    In Closing 45

4 Consolidating Authority Amidst Oppositions 47
Gospelizing 47
Socio-Economic Argument 49
Parental Authority 53
    A Breastfeeding Mother 53
    A Father 55
Imitation 56
In Closing 59

5 Sexualized Others and the Rhetoric of Exclusion 61
A Sexualized City? 62
"Some Guy" (τινα) 64
"Having the Father's Wife" 66
Porneia 68
Kill the Sinner! 70
In Closing 73

6 The Politics of Many Tongues 75
What Is "Speaking in Tongue(s)"? 77
Pneumatikos 79
How to Deal with Differences? 80
    Confessional Framework (12:1-3) 80
    Theological Framework (12:4-11) 81
    Social Body Framework (12:12-31) 81
    The Love Framework (13:1-13) 82
The Silencing of Foreign Languages 83
What Would Have Been the Corinthians' Reaction? 86
In Closing 87

Conclusion 89
Money and Politics 90
A Final Reflection 93

Bibliography 95
Index of Authors 105
Index of Subjects 107

Introduction

The Corinthians have long been burdened with a negative reputation. Commentators depict them as the embodiment of everything that can go wrong in society and the church, one of them describing the Corinthians as "filled with arrogance, seemingly supportive of immorality, involved in litigation, and struggling over sexual relations within the husband-wife relationship" (Cook III 2002: 44). David Wenham adds that the Corinthian church was mired in "gross immorality" and "fierce arguments" on topics like women's ministry, spiritual gifts, and food offered to idols. He paints a chaotic picture, suggesting that some advocated celibacy as the Christian ideal, while others denied the resurrection altogether (Wenham 1997: 137). Other scholars echo these sentiments. David Prior calls them "the notoriously messy church at Corinth" (Prior 2020: 13), and Alan F. Johnson highlights their disorder, suggesting that Paul's opening statement in 1 Corinthians 1:2 is only remarkable when we see "the messy condition" of the congregation (Johnson 2010: 37). C. K. Barrett underscores that much of what we learn from Paul's letters stems from "what the Corinthians got wrong" (Barrett 1964: 269). The list could go longer.

When one hears these scholarly opinions about the Corinthians, the conclusion seems straightforward: the Corinthians are bad people. Don't be like them! Paul is always right, and the Corinthians are wrong. This list of negative caricatures reinforces the idea that the Corinthians are the "other"—a group from whom we, as modern readers, must distance ourselves. But why have the Corinthians been saddled with this reputation? Before diving into 1 Corinthians, it's important to address some key interpretive issues.

One of the central issues is that the Corinthians are voiceless—we do not hear their perspective directly. Scholars frequently compare reading Paul's letters to overhearing a one-sided phone conversation (Barclay 1962: xv; Keck 1979: vii; Johnston 2013: 274; Gorman 2017: 94; Peterson 2021: 165). While this analogy is useful for illustrating the limitation of hearing only Paul's side of the dialogue, it also highlights a critical gap: given the absence of the Corinthians' voices, our understanding of the Corinthians has been shaped exclusively by Paul's portrayal of them.

Given that, unlike a typical phone conversation, Paul's letters are read and referenced by churches worldwide, influencing how Christians understand their faith and moral lives, there is all the more reason to be concerned about this absence of the Corinthians' voices. As Yii-Jan Lin puts it, "Not everyone may read ancient Greek—but millions of Christians and interested people read the Bible. Thousands of individuals and communities consume—metaphorically and literally, in ritual—the word of God" (Lin 2024: 184). For Paul's words to the Corinthians have been used to construct unjust systems of exclusion and inclusion, particularly against women, the LGBTQ community, Jewish people, enslaved people, etc. The stakes are enormous. In South Africa, for example, Christo Lombaard points out that 1 Corinthians 7:17-24 was one of "the favoured texts used in the theology of apartheid to sanction racially segregated congregations" (Lombaard 2009: 276). These texts extend far beyond their original context, shaping social, political, and religious structures. As Antoinette Clark Wire argues, in Lutheran and Reformed traditions, Paul's perspective has often been absolutized, treated as the normative theological voice (Wire 1990: 10).

The Author's Intention?

What perpetuates the hierarchical relationship between Paul and the Corinthians? Largely the overwhelming focus on authorial intention in biblical scholarship. In the summer of 2024, I gave a talk at a college in Indonesia about the crucial role of *readers* in the process of interpretation. To my surprise, many students felt disoriented because they had been taught that the only legitimate way to read was by searching for the *author's* intention. Introducing the concept of readers' involvement shook the very foundation of their understanding of hermeneutics. This confusion stems from the fact that many hermeneutics courses fail to expose students to the complexity of the interpretative process. Professors and clergy typically teach students and church members that the meaning of a text can only be uncovered by attempting to access the author's state of mind, as if the text were merely and simply transparent window into the author's intentions. Within this interpretive framework, exegetes often consider the task of interpretation to entail nothing beyond uncovering the author's intended meaning. This becomes the ultimate goal of interpretation.

The scholarly focus on authorial intention in biblical interpretation is, in fact, a relatively new phenomenon, traceable to nineteenth-century German Romanticism. The Romantic tradition understood language as originating from human feeling, and thus, to understand the outward expression of language, one must examine the psychology of the person expressing it. Friedrich Schleiermacher's work on hermeneutics in the early nineteenth century developed this need for an internal inquiry into the psychological state of the author, the genius behind a text. For Schleiermacher, hermeneutics requires close attention to both the grammatical and psychological aspects of a text. As Hans-Georg Gadamer rightly points out, "Schleiermacher's particular contribution is psychological interpretation" (Gadamer 1989: 186). Schleiermacher's approach seeks to return to the origin of language production, to the inner feeling of the speaker. Interpretation, in this view, becomes an excavation into the psychological state of the author—what Gadamer refers to as "a reproduction of the original production" or "the inverse of an act of speech, the reconstruction of construction" (Gadamer 1989: 188). Schleiermacher narrows the scope of interpretation to psychology because, for him, it is "the most individual and the least common, *the original*" (Schleiermacher 1998: 13).

It is therefore not surprising that Western scholarship is almost obsessively focused on questions of authorship, evident in nearly every New Testament introduction. Debates about whether Paul wrote certain letters, for instance, have persisted since the nineteenth century. But why is this considered so crucial? This perspective views the author as the sole source of meaning, with scholars believing that by uncovering the author's intention, they can access the text's true meaning. But can they?

Scholars often refer to this method as *exegesis*—drawing out or uncovering the intended meaning of a text. They often frame this approach as the only valid way to engage with the text, believing such an approach to be objective and disinterested. For example, Gordon Fee and Douglas Stuart define exegesis as "the careful, systematic study of Scripture to discover the original, intended meaning. This is basically a historical task ... to find out what was the original intent of the words of the Bible" (Fee and Stuart 1993: 22).

This focus on discovering the "original intended meaning" has led scholars to align their interpretations with Paul's perspective in the conflict with the Corinthians. Their primary interpretative allegiance is to Paul, as the presumed author, and to uncovering his motivations and intentions.

This emphasis on authorial intent and this approach to the text often flattens its complexity. By prioritizing Paul's intentions as the key to unlocking the "correct" meaning, scholars may unintentionally (or, in some cases, conveniently and deliberately!) overlook the dynamics of power and rhetoric at play in the letter. They treat Paul's words as objective reports, rather than recognizing them as part of a larger rhetorical strategy designed to persuade and influence his audience. This way of reading, Wire correctly insists, prevents Paul "from persuading us" (Wire 1990: 10). It creates a kind of hermeneutical tunnel vision, which ignores the experiences and voices of the Corinthians in favor of Paul's singular voice.

Furthermore, some theological traditions understand Paul's words not merely as Paul's, but as God's, and more specifically as therefore inerrant, free of all mistakes. This divine endorsement often discourages readers from critically investigating Paul's portrayal of the Corinthians, reinforcing the belief that Paul's perspective is not only authoritative but divinely sanctioned. Who would dare question God? Although the Bible is filled with the stories of people questioning and wrestling with God, the modern interpretation of Paul often discourages readers from wrestling with Paul. This theological tendency inevitably absolutizes Paul's discourse. Such an approach narrows the possibilities for understanding the text, leaving little room for alternative viewpoints, including those of the Corinthians themselves. It often dismisses the voices Paul critiques, treated them as having no legitimacy of their own, existing solely to highlight Paul's correctness.

The issue of authorial intention is far more complex than it might initially appear. Since Paul is no longer present to clarify what he "meant," we are left solely with his writings, which have taken on a life of their own. Across history and diverse geographic contexts, Paul's words have been continuously reshaped and reinterpreted through layers of scholarship, tradition, and theological reflection, often extending well beyond what he may have originally intended. While the search for authorial intention often stems from a desire for certainty and objectivity, it becomes a tenuous endeavor in the absence of the author. When scholars claim to have uncovered Paul's intention, they frequently project their own perspectives onto Paul, though this projection is seldom acknowledged in academic discourse. It is no surprise, then, that countless commentaries on Paul have emerged over the centuries. But which, if any, truly capture Paul's original intent? Ultimately, the subjective lens of the interpreter shapes any claim to understanding Paul's intention. Every act of *ex*egesis, in this sense, is inherently *eis*egesis.

As Paul's letters circulated among early Christian communities, the interpretations of these texts inevitably varied based on the readers' diverse social locations, experiences, and cultural contexts. In other words, Paul's text is already an intersubjective artifact, existing outside of Paul in a social space where intersubjective, dialogical interactions occur (Bakhtin 2004: 282). The meanings derived from these letters were not fixed or singular but conditionally constructed by those who encountered the text. Indeed, interpretation is never neutral or objective; instead, it is shaped by the readers' particular worldview and historical situatedness.

The Corinthian "Slogans"

How, then, can we get at what the Corinthians' really believed and did? One of the primary ways in which scholars have attempted to reconstruct the beliefs and behaviors of the Corinthians is by analyzing the slogans Paul attributes to them throughout his letter. These slogans are typically understood as phrases or ideas that Paul quotes and then refutes. Scholars often interpret them as evidence of the Corinthians' misguided beliefs, which, of course, Paul seeks to correct. Consider an example from 1 Corinthians 6:12, as it appears in the NRSV:

> "All things are lawful for me," but not all things are beneficial. "All things are lawful for me," but I will not be dominated by anything. "Food is meant for the stomach and the stomach for food," and God will destroy both one and the other. The body is meant not for fornication but for the Lord, and the Lord for the body.

Notice how two clauses are placed in quotation marks. The first is "all things are lawful for me." This clause appears three times in 1 Corinthians, twice here and then in 10:23 (without "for me"). And the second such clause is "food is meant for the stomach and the stomach for food." Why are they in quotation marks? According to the NRSV and many Pauline scholars (Murphy-O'Connor 1978; Burk 2008; Smith 2008), these phrases are not Paul's own words but those of the Corinthians. Even Michael Goulder contends more specifically that the pronoun "me" refers to the man who has his father's woman in 5:1 (Goulder 1999: 348). Those scholars insist that Paul could not possibly endorse such statements. The so-called libertines (here a derogatory term) are the Corinthians, not Paul. This is ironically inconsistent in light of the Corinthians' statement that Paul quotes in 7:1, "It is well for a man not to touch a woman," indicating that they *might* have a restrictive view of sexuality.

Paul does not explicitly indicate that the statements in question are the words of the Corinthians. In contrast to 1:11, where he clearly signals that he is quoting them by prefacing the sayings with "each of you says," no such explicit marker appears in chapter 6. Yet, many scholars continue to assert that these are the Corinthians' slogans. By attributing these statements to the Corinthians, scholars may appear to be giving them a voice, but this often serves the scholars' underlying purpose of discrediting them, portraying them in a negative light. This interpretive approach tends to extend the benefit of doubt to Paul, while consistently casting the Corinthians in an unfavorable light. Consequently, the supposed voice given to the Corinthians only reinforces their perceived moral and theological deficiencies.

But what if these statements are not the Corinthians' slogans at all? What if Paul is merely expressing his own conviction about Christian freedom, a conviction that might originally have had nothing to do with *porneia* (Goulder 1999: 344–5)? What if the Corinthians are actually grappling with such an extreme view? Jonathan Rivett Robinson is one of the lone voices to argue that attributing these statements to the Corinthians is textually unnecessary. He points out the need for modern scholars to avoid "the risk of mistaking Paul's words for the Corinthians" (Robinson 2018: 148). Paul, he insists, is capable of signaling a citation if he deems it necessary (Robinson 2018: 149). Furthermore, the concept of freedom in Christ is present in Paul's other writings, such as Galatians and Romans. In the case of 1 Corinthians 6, Paul could be stating his own belief that "everything is permissible" before clarifying his position by adding "but not all things are beneficial." In doing so, he could be refining his own thoughts on Christian freedom.

Even if we grant that these slogans did originate from the Corinthians, we must approach Paul's representation of them with caution and avoid accepting them at face value. Paul may be misrepresenting or oversimplifying the Corinthians' beliefs to strengthen his argument. The slogan "All things are lawful for me" may not reflect a reckless embrace of moral license, as Paul seems to suggest: it could represent the Corinthians' understanding of freedom—specifically the belief that such freedom is achieved through Christ, which is similar to what Paul himself believes (2 Cor. 3:17; Gal. 5:1; 5:13; Rom. 6:18-22; 8:1-2).

In this light, Paul's response is not merely a straightforward correction of their beliefs but may also be a rhetorical strategy aimed at reasserting his authority and control over the community. By framing their understanding of freedom as dangerously misguided, Paul positions himself as the one with the correct interpretation of religious life, ensuring that his voice remains dominant in guiding the church. As we will see in Chapter 3, this suggests that Paul's engagement with the Corinthians is not only theological but also political, involving a contest over whose voice and interpretation should hold the most influence within the community. Therefore, interpreting these slogans requires a critical lens, a recognition that Paul, like any writer, is advancing his own perspective and may be framing the Corinthians' beliefs in a way that best supports his theological and political objectives.

To grasp fully the dynamics at play, we must remain open to the possibility that the Corinthians held a more nuanced understanding of freedom than Paul's representation suggests, and that their position, while different from Paul's, may not have been as reckless as he implies. Such an approach invites us to consider the complexities of early Jesus-following communities, where differing interpretations of faith and practice coexisted and often created tension. Rather than accepting Paul's portrayal as the definitive account, students of the New Testament should recognize the rhetorical dimensions of his letters and remain attuned to the possible motivations behind how he represents his opponents' views. In doing so, we gain a better understanding of the theological and social dynamics among the early followers of Jesus.

Re-presentation

Edward Said's exploration of literature as a form of representation, particularly in his influential book, *Orientalism*, is pivotal for understanding how cultural discourse is shaped. Said argues that Western literature about the Orient is not an objective truth and a reality itself, but rather a series of representations—interpretations and constructs that emerge from specific cultural and political contexts (Said 2003: 10). He highlights that the production of knowledge is inherently mediated through language, meaning that literature does not present reality as it is but rather *re*-presents it through various filters of power, ideology, and perception. Or as Elisabeth Schüssler Fiorenza describes it, "All representations of the world are informed by our own historical-cultural position, by values and practices rooted in them, and by the ways we are implicated in power-relations" (Schüssler Fiorenza 1989: 24).

This framework of representation, which critiques the ways in which power and discourse shape the construction of the other, can also be applied to biblical texts, including Paul's letters. Like Western literature about the Orient, Paul's writings represent rather than merely describe reality. They are mediated through Paul's cultural, theological, and personal biases. For example, when Paul refers to the Corinthians as his "beloved children" (1 Cor. 4:14), we must ask: Is Paul's statement a literal description, or is he constructing a re-presentation of the Corinthians in a way that serves his rhetorical purposes? Do the Corinthians accept this characterization, or do they resist it? What does this representation reveal about Paul himself?

This approach opens the door to a deeper understanding of 1 Corinthians as a text shaped by Paul's personal, cultural, and theological perspectives. His letters are not neutral records of historical facts or interactions, but are rhetorical constructs designed to shape his audience's behavior and beliefs. In this light, Paul's representations of the Corinthians can be understood as attempts to assert control over their behavior, both in terms of moral conduct and theological alignment. Thus, Paul's descriptions of the Corinthians should not be taken as objective realities but as part of a larger rhetorical strategy aimed at persuading his readers to follow his leadership—a topic we will explore further in later chapters.

Paul's portrayal of the Corinthians also reveals a deeper struggle for authority within the early Christian movement. By depicting the Corinthians as immoral or misguided, Paul positions himself as the enlightened apostle and true guide, while casting the Corinthians as wayward followers in need of correction. His paternalistic tone, particularly in passages like 1 Corinthians 4:14-17, where he refers to the Corinthians as his "beloved children" and urges them to imitate him, reinforces a hierarchical relationship. In this framing, Paul is the wise, experienced father, and the Corinthians are immature, rebellious children who need guidance and discipline. As Mitzi Smith puts it, "Paul can be, and too often is, problematic without being misread" (Smith 2023: 9).

The Corinthians, as Paul represents them in 1 Corinthians, are a group of people beset by moral, theological, and social issues. But we must ask: Are these issues really as Paul describes them, or are they Paul's interpretations of what is happening in the Corinthian community? Do the Corinthians have their own theological reasoning and cultural rationale for their actions, and is Paul dismissing or misrepresenting these reasons?

These questions become particularly relevant when we consider how Paul addresses issues like sexuality and social divisions in 1 Corinthians. For example, in 1 Corinthians 5, Paul condemns a member of the Corinthian community for sexual immorality (*porneia*), specifically for having his father's wife. This is presented as a clear violation of moral standards, and Paul urges the community to expel the offender. But is it possible that Paul does not fully understand the situation? Could this issue be based on a rumor or misunderstanding? What if the community had a different understanding of what constituted appropriate sexual behavior, shaped by their own cultural and religious context? These questions challenge us to think from the other side, to be sympathetic to the Corinthians' perspective, and to engage more deeply with the complex dynamics at play.

Rather than taking Paul's representation at face value, what if we were to consider that the Corinthians had legitimate reasons for their actions and beliefs? What if they were to question this paternalistic framing? What if their supposed immorality and disorder were actually creative ways of navigating the complex social and religious dynamics of their time? By viewing the Corinthians as active agents rather than passive recipients of Paul's critique, we can begin to see the power dynamics at play in Paul's letters more clearly. This approach invites us to read 1 Corinthians "beyond the heroic Paul," to borrow the words of Melanie Johnson-DeBaufre and LauraNasrallah (Johnson-DeBaufre and Nasrallah 2011).

Sympathetic Reading

Because a text exists within a web of complex power relations—not only between Paul and the Corinthians but also between Paul and his readers across time—I propose that we approach the text as "sympathetic" readers. Allow me to elaborate on this concept with the help of Adele Reinhartz, a Jewish scholar of the New Testament, who has carefully examined the troubling portrayal of the Jews in the Gospel of John. In her study, Reinhartz identifies four distinct ways of reading this gospel: a compliant reading, a resistant reading, a sympathetic reading, and an engaged reading (Reinhartz 2002, 2009).

A compliant reading is one that agrees entirely with the text, accepting its claims without question. A resistant reading, on the other hand, pushes back against the text, challenging its claims and assumptions. A sympathetic reading, which Reinhartz herself undertakes, entails temporarily setting aside personal identifications—in her case, with the Jews of the Gospel of John—in order to understand sympathetically the gospel's logic and its historical and textual contexts. This strategy involves first exploring the text's intrinsic reasoning before applying critical evaluation.

Finally, Reinhartz introduces the concept of an "engaged reading." As she puts it, "As an engaged reader, I finally sat across the table from the

Beloved Disciple. I stared directly at him and also allowed myself to see my own reflection in his eyes" (Reinhartz 2002: 162). This kind of reading goes beyond simply understanding the text; it involves a critical dialog with it. The engaged reader does not merely absorb or reject the text but actively responds to it—talking back, questioning, and allowing their personal context to interact with the text in a meaningful way. In this sense, the text becomes a living dialog between reader and writer, one that acknowledges both historical distance and contemporary relevance.

While Reinhartz's framework of engaged reading informs my approach—and I would argue that every reading is, in some sense, engaged—her framework helps differentiate various reading gestures for analytical purposes. My approach, however, does not aim to immerse the reader—you, in this case—in engaged reading right away. Engaged reading is deeply particular and depends on the social location of each reader. My engagement with 1 Corinthians will inevitably differ from yours, as each of us brings unique perspectives, experiences, and backgrounds to the text. What I may find challenging or affirming might not resonate in the same way for you. For this reason, I believe that an engaged reading requires a solid foundation in sympathetic reading. Without first attempting to understand the text sympathetically within its historical, cultural, and political complexities, it is difficult to engage with it meaningfully. Sympathetic reading provides the necessary groundwork, offering an entry point to grapple with the deeper layers of the text before responding to it from our own social location.

In guiding you through 1 Corinthians in this book, my aim is to equip you with the tools to read the text sympathetically, helping you understand its internal logic, historical context, and political dynamics. I hope that, in time, you will become an engaged reader. While Reinhartz's sympathetic reading involves showing sympathy toward the Beloved Disciple, this book encourages you to extend that sympathy not only to Paul but also to the Corinthians. The word "sympathy" comes from two Greek words: *syn* (with, together) and *pathos* (emotion, feeling, or experience). To be sympathetic is to try to feel or experience with another. To date, scholars have typically extended their sympathy primarily to Paul. However, it is equally important—and fair—to extend our sympathy to the Corinthians as well. By sympathetically understanding the text from both perspectives, you can engage more fully and nuance the dialog within the letter. This dual sympathy opens new avenues for grasping the complexities of the interactions and tensions between Paul and the Corinthian community.

The Plan of the Book

Rather than provide an exhaustive discussion of all the debates surrounding 1 Corinthians, this book's primary goal is to guide readers toward becoming more empathetic interpreters of a letter filled with polemical issues. As a deeply polemical text, 1 Corinthians invites diverse interpretations. This book encourages you to imagine how the Corinthians themselves might have received Paul's letter, particularly in the context of their political and social struggles. My hope is that you will move beyond being a passive recipient of Paul's rhetoric and instead actively engage with his arguments, addressing his concerns directly. The following is the plan of the book.

Chapter 1 highlights the importance of Paul's letters in the New Testament, particularly his correspondence with the Corinthians. It explains the formal structure of ancient letter writing and the challenges of communication in that era. The chapter focuses on Paul's strained relationship with the Corinthians, who questioned his authority. Paul's letter to them addresses various issues in response to reports and letters from the community. The chapter underscores how indirect information shaped Paul's responses and it highlights the difficulty in reconstructing the Corinthians' perspective based solely on Paul's account.

Chapter 2 provides a roadmap for navigating 1 Corinthians. It highlights key themes such as Paul's defense of his authority, moral issues, advice on marriage, idol food, spiritual gifts, and the resurrection. The chapter also explores the context of Roman Corinth, a city rebuilt after its destruction in 146 BCE and characterized by social diversity, economic inequality, and religious plurality. Corinth's hybrid identity, shaped by both Greek and Roman influences, created challenges and opportunities for the early Christian community. Understanding this context is essential for interpreting Paul's letters to the Corinthians.

Chapter 3 examines Paul's complex relationship with the Corinthian church, focusing on the challenge to his authority. While Acts portrays Paul's ministry in Corinth as initially successful, Paul's letters, particularly 1 Corinthians, reveal tensions within the community. Paul responds to reports from Chloe's people about divisions among the Corinthians, who were aligning themselves with different leaders, including Apollos and Cephas. The chapter emphasizes that the primary issue was not just factionalism but the Corinthians' rejection of Paul's authority. Paul's strategy was to reassert his leadership by shifting focus from ritual acts like baptism to the proclamation of the gospel, framing his authority in terms of preaching rather than hierarchy. Ultimately, Paul's letter reflects a broader struggle over leadership in a community where his influence had waned.

Chapter 4 examines Paul's struggle to assert authority in the Corinthian church amid opposition. He urges unity to reinforce his leadership, focusing on the cross as the core of the gospel, which clashed with the Corinthians' preference for power and success. Paul connects their socioeconomic status to the "foolishness" of the cross, reminding them of their humble calling. Using parental metaphors, Paul positions himself as both mother and father, commanding the Corinthians to imitate him to strengthen his control. Yet this approach may have alienated some in Corinth's diverse community, revealing the challenge of maintaining authority while navigating social and cultural differences.

Chapter 5 explores the idea of the "sexualized other" through Paul's critique in 1 Corinthians 5, where he accuses a Corinthian man of sexual immorality. The chapter examines how Paul weaponizes vague, second-hand information to portray the man and the Corinthian assembly negatively. Paul's demand for the man's expulsion, and even death, to preserve the church's purity reflects a paternalistic and exclusionary approach to leadership that alienates the community.

Chapter 6 addresses the politics of language in 1 Corinthians 12–14. In Roman Corinth, a city filled with immigrants, Paul's discomfort with the disorderliness of speaking in tongues reflects a desire to control linguistic diversity in the church. Paul insists that foreign languages be translated during worship or otherwise silenced, prioritizing unity and order over diversity. The chapter concludes by analyzing how Paul's theology intertwines with his views on social order, using religious authority to manage the multilingual reality of the Corinthian assembly.

In short, as we journey through this book and these ideas, it is important to keep in mind that understanding a text like 1 Corinthians requires more than simply receiving Paul's words; it demands a critical and empathetic engagement with both Paul's arguments and the experiences of the Corinthians themselves. This process of interpretation invites us to question, challenge, and reimagine the power dynamics at play in the text. As Sara Ahmed reminds us, "the purpose of reading is to be critical and to question" (Ahmed 1999: 18). By approaching 1 Corinthians with a critical eye and an open mind, this book aims to deepen your understanding of the text and its broader implications—both for the early Christian community and for us today.

1

Paul's Correspondence with the Corinthians

Letters are central to the New Testament. Of its twenty-seven books, twenty-one are letters, with the majority written by Paul (or influenced by him). These letters were essential for communication and instruction in the early Christian movements, as they provided guidance, theological reflections, exhortations, and practical solutions to various issues facing the fledgling Christian communities. Letters were not only a form of personal communication but also public documents that addressed whole communities. Paul's letters are a prime example of this, especially his correspondence with the Corinthians, a correspondence that reflects the complexities of his relationship with them.

An Ancient Letter

In the ancient world, letter writing was a far more labor-intensive process than it is today. Letters were handwritten, often by a professional scribe or secretary (ἀμανουησίς), and delivered by trusted couriers, many of whom were enslaved individuals (see Moss 2024, 2023). This process was both costly and time-consuming. Depending on the distance and the available methods of transportation, a letter could take months to reach its destination (Klauck 2006: 61–6). Unlike modern communication through email or instant messaging, which allows for immediate feedback, correspondence in the ancient world was slow and deliberate. This context adds significance to the letters in the New Testament, as they were likely composed with great care, given that any misunderstandings could take months or even years to resolve or undo.

In modern communication, emails typically start with salutations such as "Dear ..., " or "Hi ..., " whereas first-century letters adhered to a different convention. The greeting formula often followed the pattern of

"From A to B, greetings!" (Stowers 1986: 21). This pattern is evident in the opening of 1 Corinthians:

A) Paul, called to be an apostle of Christ Jesus by the will of God, and our brother Sosthenes,

B) To the church of God that is in Corinth, to those who are sanctified in Christ Jesus, called to be saints, together with all those who in every place call on the name of our Lord Jesus Christ, both their Lord and ours:

Greetings: Grace to you and peace from God our Father and the Lord Jesus Christ.

(1 Cor. 1:1-3)[1]

Paul follows this epistolary convention. While the typical salutation in ancient letters is χαίρειν or χαῖρε (Tite 2010: 62), Paul uses the expression "Grace to you and peace ... (χάρις ὑμῖν καὶ εἰρήνη)," which also appears in his other letters (Rom. 1:7; 2 Cor. 1:2; Gal. 1:3; Phil. 1:2; 1 Thess. 1:1; Philemon 3). The formula is also present in the so-called disputed letters—letters whose alleged Pauline authorship scholars question (Eph. 1:2; Col. 1:2; 2 Thess. 1:2; Tit. 1:2), with a slight variation adding "mercy" in 1 and 2 Timothy.

Paul frequently includes co-authors in his letters (cf. Phil. 1:1; 1 Thess. 1:1; 2 Cor. 1:1), and 1 Corinthians is no exception, where he names Sosthenes as a co-author. The name Sosthenes was common in the Greek world, but who exactly was this man? The name appears in Acts 18:17, to identify the synagogue leader who was violently beaten before the tribunal in Corinth. The identity of those responsible for the violence is ambiguous, as Acts only states "all" (πάντες). Some ancient scribes added "the Greeks," while others wrote "the Jews," reflecting disagreement among early interpreters. However, it remains uncertain whether the Sosthenes in Acts is the same individual mentioned in 1 Corinthians. In any case, in both texts, Sosthenes remains an enigmatic figure. Paul never mentions him again after the letter's opening, referring to him simply as "the brother" (ὁ ἀδελφὸς), suggesting he may have been a believer known to the Corinthians (Collins 1999: 42; Fitzmyer 2008: 121). His role in the letter remains speculative. Fee proposes that Sosthenes may have served as Paul's secretary, though he concedes, "that too is conjecture" (Fee 1988: 31).

If Sosthenes did serve as Paul's secretary (ἀμανουησίς), that raises important questions about his social status. Candida Moss's recent research highlights the significant role enslaved workers played in the production

---

[1] All biblical quotations in this book are taken from the New Revised Standard Version (NRSV), unless otherwise noted.

of the New Testament. "As uncomfortable as it may be to think about, the spread of Christianity was assisted by Roman roads and Roman human trafficking," Moss observes (Moss 2024). Could Sosthenes have been an enslaved person, whose name was briefly mentioned and never reappeared? Just as Paul calls Onesimus "a brother" (Phil. 16), is it possible that Sosthenes was likewise an enslaved person referred to as "the brother"?

In this introduction, Paul also describes himself as "an apostle of Christ Jesus by the will of God." Claiming his apostleship as divinely appointed is a significant power move at the beginning of the letter. For as we will explore later, at this time the Corinthian community was questioning Paul's authority, and so was turning to other leaders. This made it particularly crucial for Paul to establish from the outset that his authority was divinely sanctioned. The writer of the letter attributes this divine calling solely to Paul, not to Sosthenes, the inference being that challenging Paul means challenging God. As Fee notes:

> The Corinthians are a church at odds with their founder: they are judging him (4:1–5) and examining him as to his apostleship (9:1–23). Later (4:15; 9:1–2) he will present further evidence for his apostleship (he founded the church; he saw the Risen Lord), but because this church is questioning that apostleship, he begins by asserting its divine origins.
> (Fee 1988: 28)

Furthermore, letters in the ancient world were written not only for personal reasons, such as staying connected with loved ones, but also for public purposes. In fact, the distinction between private and public letters was often blurred, as these categories frequently overlapped (Stowers 1986). First Corinthians, for example, was written for a communal audience—a group of people. As John Muir observes:

> The New Testament letters may fit into a recognizable context, but it is certain that they also mark the beginnings of a new genre; they are at the start of a tradition in which church leaders, a little like the Hellenistic kings before them, used more or less public letters to dispense important advice on community management, doctrine, instruction, exhortation, and discipline, as well as more mundane matters of administration.
> (Muir 2012: 275)

The recipient of this letter is clearly a community: "To the church of God that is in Corinth." In 1 Corinthians 5:4, Paul mentions that he is present in spirit with the Corinthians when they gather together. Margaret Mitchell rightly suspects that Paul "assumes they will read his letter collectively, perhaps in a liturgical setting, or some other corporate context wherein [his] disciplinary sentence could be pronounced, and an offender cast out"

(Mitchell 2003: 43). It is not surprising, then, that Paul uses the second-person plural pronoun (ὑμεῖς) far more often than the singular (σύ) in 1 Corinthians. The second-person singular pronoun σύ appears only seven times over the course of the letter (4:7; 7:21; 8:10; 12:21; 14:17; 15:36, 55), whereas ὑμεῖς occurs over a hundred times. Thus, when one encounters the pronoun "you" in English translations of 1 Corinthians, it is typically plural. Paul is addressing a community that has become estranged from him.

The Correspondence

First Corinthians is not Paul's only letter to the Corinthians. In addition to the two letters we have now in the New Testament, there were likely several other letters exchanged between Paul and the Corinthians. In 1 Corinthians 5:9, Paul references a previous letter in which he instructed the community about dealing with πόρνοις—a term related to sexual immorality—an issue we will explore in more depth later in this book. That letter could very well have been Paul's first correspondence with the Corinthians, but its fate is unknown; it is presumed lost.

After sending this first letter, the Corinthians responded by writing back to Paul. However, it remains unclear whether their letter was a direct reply or part of an ongoing dialog. We find evidence of their communication in 1 Corinthians 7:1, where Paul notes their inquiry regarding a specific teaching: "it is well for a man not to touch a woman." They were seeking Paul's authoritative opinion on this matter. As Helen Bond observes, "Quite clearly the community was loyal enough to Paul to put their queries and concerns to him (perhaps at the instigation of Chloe and Stephanas), but there are signs that Paul's authority was already being challenged among some circles within a year or so of his departure" (Bond 2003: 192). Despite growing divisions, there were still members of the Corinthian assembly who respected Paul and sought his guidance, even as others began to challenge his authority.

At the conclusion of 1 Corinthians, Paul expresses his intention to visit Corinth on his way to Macedonia, planning to spend the winter with the community there (16:5-7). He writes, "I do not want to see you now just in passing, for I hope to spend some time with you, if the Lord permits. But I will stay in Ephesus until Pentecost" (1 Cor. 16:7-8a). Paul was residing in Ephesus (cf. Acts 19) when he penned 1 Corinthians after receiving their letter and learning of the many issues facing the church through Chloe's people (1 Cor. 1:12). Yet, not everyone in Corinth believed that Paul would return, and some even doubted his intentions, claiming he would not follow through on his promise to visit (4:18). Scholars generally agree that approximately four to five years had passed between Paul's initial departure from Corinth and the writing of 1 Corinthians, though there is still some debate on this timeline (Horrell 2000: 88).

During this interval of several years, Paul's relationship with the Corinthians had become strained. Some members of the community had begun rejecting his authority, turning to other teachers, and dismissing his guidance. Paul's frustration is palpable in the letter; he even threatens to come to them "with a rod" if they do not change their ways (4:21), suggesting that he was prepared to assert his authority more forcefully if necessary. Paul's leadership philosophy, which emphasized the need for the Corinthians to "imitate me!" (4:16), was not well-received by some in the assembly. In response to the growing tensions, Paul sent Timothy to Corinth, likely as the bearer of the 1 Corinthians letter (16:10), hoping that Timothy could remind them of Paul's teachings and authority (4:17). In many respects, Timothy served as a mediator between Paul and the Corinthians, trying to bridge the gap and restore some semblance of unity. However, Paul also hoped to send Apollos, another respected teacher, but for reasons unknown, Apollos refused to go (16:12), leaving Paul to rely on Timothy.

Unfortunately, Timothy's visit seems to have been largely unsuccessful, as it did not resolve the underlying tensions in Corinth. Despite Paul's best efforts to reconcile with the community, the conflict persisted, leading him to make the promised visit in person. However, this visit proved to be disastrous, resulting in what Paul later referred to as a "painful visit" (2 Cor. 2:1). During this time, the divisions between Paul and the Corinthians deepened, and the visit left Paul feeling profound distressed and sorrowful. Reflecting on his emotional state, Paul wrote, "For even when we came into Macedonia, our bodies had no rest, but we were afflicted in every way—disputes without and fears within" (2 Cor. 7:5). After leaving Corinth, Paul wrote another letter to the church, one filled with deep emotional pain. He described it as written "out of much distress and anguish of heart and with many tears" (2 Cor. 2:4; cf. 7:8). This so-called tearful letter has been the subject of much scholarly speculation. Some scholars argue that this letter may be preserved within 2 Corinthians, particularly in chapter 10 to 13 (Kennedy 1897; Brown 1997), although this remains a topic of ongoing debate (Watson 1984; Welborn 1995). If this letter is indeed found in 2 Corinthians 10–13, it reveals Paul's deep grievance against the "super-apostles" (2 Cor. 11:5) and his frustrations with those Corinthians who mocked him for his weak physical presence, despite the strength of his letters (2 Cor. 10:10).

In short, 1 Corinthians is likely Paul's second letter to the Corinthians, not his first. It is likely that Paul and the Corinthians exchanged several letters, letters reflecting the complex and evolving nature of their relationship. Unfortunately, we now possess only two of these letters: 1 Corinthians and 2 Corinthians. This correspondence, however, offers valuable insight into the fraught relationship between Paul and the Corinthian church, one marked by rejection, disobedience, and ongoing conflict. As we turn to examine the structure of 1 Corinthians, it is important to read it with an awareness of this rocky background.

The Structure of 1 Corinthians

First Corinthians is a complex letter, interwoven with numerous theological, cultural, social, and political issues. Remember also that Paul was not physically present in Corinth when he wrote this letter. He composed it after leaving the city, meaning he addressed the Corinthians from a distance, attempting to guide them through written instructions rather than face-to-face interaction. Though Paul clearly had a relationship with the Corinthian community, the geographical distance meant he had to rely on indirect sources of information to understand their situation. As John Hurd observes, "1 Corinthians is not based on the actual state of affairs in Corinth but on what Paul believed to have been the situation there" (Hurd 1983: 61). Hurd further argues that Paul gathered his information from two primary sources: (1) an oral report from Chloe's people, and (2) a written letter the Corinthians had sent him.

However, categorizing the report from Chloe's people as strictly "word of mouth information" (Hurd 1983: 62) may be an oversimplification. The term "hearing" in 1 Corinthians 1:11 does not explicitly indicate that the report was oral. In fact, "hearing" doesn't necessarily imply oral communication, as seen in passages like 1 John 2:7 and Revelation. 22:18. Chloe's people may have communicated with Paul via a letter or other written medium. Therefore, Paul's information could have come through either oral or written channels. What is clear is that Paul relied on *secondary* sources to learn about the situation in Corinth.

Hurd also points to the use of the phrase περὶ δέ—which appears six times in 1 Corinthians (7:1, 25; 8:1; 12:1; 16:1, 12) and often translated as "now concerning"—as evidence that Paul was responding to a written letter from the Corinthians. His argument is based on the connection between περὶ δέ and the verb γράφω in 1 Corinthians 7:1. According to Hurd, this formula "appears to consist of an answer to a question or questions asked by the Corinthian church" (Hurd 1983: 64). However, Margaret Mitchell has convincingly demonstrated that within the broader context of Greek literary culture, περὶ δέ does not necessarily indicate a response to a written source (Mitchell 1989: 255). In other words, we cannot use περὶ δέ as definitive proof that Paul's responses in the second half of the letter were based on a written letter from the Corinthians. As Mitchell argues, "Despite the fact that in itself περὶ δέ can tell us nothing of the source or order of these topics, it is our most important clue to understanding how Paul, on his own terms, chose to respond to the multifaceted situation at Corinth which he had been informed about" (Mitchell 1989: 256). Therefore, περὶ δέ serves more as a discursive marker, highlighting transitions between topics, rather than as a clue for identifying the source of information.

It is also noteworthy that περὶ δέ appears only in the second half of the letter (Hurd 1983: 63), for this provides an important insight into how

Paul constructs his arguments. Since περὶ δέ does not necessarily indicate a response to a written letter, but rather to "some element of their shared experience" (Mitchell 1989: 256), the phrase suggests that Paul's interaction with the Corinthians in the second half of the letter (chapter 7–16) involves topics with which he had more direct engagement or knowledge. By contrast, the first half of the letter (chapters 1–6) appears to be based on the reports he received from Chloe's people, suggesting he had only indirect knowledge of the issues at hand. This distinction leads to a division of Paul's sources: *indirect* (chapters 1–6) and *direct* (chapter 7–16).

One crucial point to consider with regard to the literary complexity of this letter is Paul's discussion of the Lord's Supper in chapter 11, where he writes, "when you come together as a church, I hear that there are divisions (σχίσματα) among you, and to some extent I believe it" (11:18). This statement shows that even in the second half of the letter Paul is not relying solely on direct knowledge of the situation. Although the division between chapters 1–6 and 7–16 may seem clear, Paul remains flexible in weaving together the various pieces of information he received, both direct and indirect, as he crafted this letter.

In conclusion, while there are distinct differences in how Paul addresses the topics in the first and second halves of 1 Corinthians, with chapters 1 to 6 being a response to reports from Chloe's people and chapter 7 to 16 engaging with topics the Corinthians themselves raised, the letter as a whole reflects a dynamic interplay of sources and perspectives. Paul's complex relationship with the Corinthians, marked by distance, mediation, and indirect knowledge, shapes the content and structure of the letter, underscoring the intricate nature of their communication. With this understanding in place, we can now turn to a deeper analysis of the letter's theological and practical concerns.

Given the above discussion, we can divide 1 Corinthians into four main sections: (1) Opening, (2) Response to an indirect source, (3) Response to a direct source, and (4) Closing.

Below is the detailed structure of the letter:

1 **Opening Section (1:1-9)**
   a. Salutation (1:1-3)
   b. Thanksgiving (1:4-9)

2 **Response to an Indirect Source (1:10–6:20)**
   a. Statements on divisions in Corinth (1:10-17)
   b. Defense of Paul's message of the cross (1:18–2:16)
   c. Further discussion on conflicts in Corinth (3:1-23)
   d. Defense of Paul's apostleship (4:1-20)
   e. The problem of *porneia* (5:1-13)
   f. Internal disputes (6:1-11)
   g. *Porneia* and the body revisited (6:12-20)

3. Response to a Direct Source (7:1–16:4)
   a. Concerning marriage (7:1-24)
   b. Concerning the unmarried (7:25-40)
   c. Concerning food sacrificed to idols (8:1–11:1)
   d. Concerning gender hierarchy (11:2-16)
   e. Concerning the Lord's Supper (11:17-34)
   f. Concerning spiritual gifts (12:1–14:40)
   g. Concerning the resurrection (15:1-58)
   h. Concerning the collection (16:1-4)

4. Closing Section (16:5-24)
   a. Travel plans (16:5-14)
   b. Greetings (16:15-24)

First, it is important to note that 1 Corinthians is not a systematic theology text. Paul's intention is not to develop a coherent theological system; his letter reflects the immediate concerns of the Corinthian community rather than a neatly organized set of doctrines. Scholarly debates about whether 1 Corinthians is a single letter or a compilation of multiple letters stem from an expectation that authors must present a coherent and unified argument. However, life is messy, and Paul's letter reveals the messiness of both his relationship with the Corinthians and the complex social and theological issues they faced. We should therefore understand this letter as Paul's ad hoc responses to the diverse problems that arose in Corinth, informed by the reports from Chloe's people, the Corinthians' own letter, and possibly other sources. His thoughts are often reactive and shaped by the specific concerns of the moment.

Second, as we will explore in the next chapter, Paul's reliance on second-hand information, particularly in the first part of the letter, leads to a passionate confrontation with the Corinthians. He heard reports that they had rejected him and were turning to other leaders, challenging his authority and teachings. As Fee rightly notes, "They stand against him on almost every issue. The key issue here is their calling his authority into question" (Fee 1988: 8). This tension underscores the deeply personal nature of Paul's engagement with the Corinthians. His identity as an apostle is at stake, and his response reveals the politics of identity, as his personal authority and position are being questioned within the broader context of the community.

Third, in light of the personal nature of Paul's confrontation, it is important to recognize that the Corinthians represent a broader spectrum of voices within early followers of Jesus. They offer a window into the diversity of beliefs and practices among these communities. Yet, their voices are often overshadowed by Paul's own narrative. Modern readers, following Paul's lead, tend to focus on his perspective and downplay the dissenting views present within the Corinthian community. One of the central challenges in reading 1 Corinthians is to reconstruct the Corinthians' beliefs and behaviors based on Paul's portrayal of them. What complicates this process further is the fact that Paul's knowledge of the Corinthians is, in part, derived from secondary sources. This creates multiple layers of representation, with Paul's filtered understanding shaping how we perceive the Corinthians.

In Closing

The correspondence between Paul and the Corinthians offers us a unique insight into the complexities of early Christian communities and the struggles over leadership, authority, and communal identity. Paul's letters, particularly 1 Corinthians, provide us with a lens through which we can examine the evolving dynamics of his relationship with this community. While Paul's apostolic authority is at the center of much of the conflict, the voices of the Corinthians—though mediated through Paul's letters—reveal a diversity of thought, practice, and resistance that shaped their engagement with Paul's teachings.

As we have seen, the structure of 1 Corinthians reflects Paul's response to both indirect reports and direct inquiries from the Corinthians, weaving together various issues that troubled the community. These issues ranged from internal disputes to theological concerns, all of which underscore the tensions within this fragile relationship. However, the letter is not merely a window into Paul's mind; it also provides us with glimpses into the lives of the Corinthians themselves.

It is important to keep in mind, as we move forward, the fragmented nature of this relationship and how Paul's letters are shaped by second-hand information and personal grievances. In the next chapter, we will look more closely at the content of the letter and the historical background against which it was written, as we continue to explore the dynamics of Paul's engagement with the Corinthian assembly.

2

Guiding the Way: An Overview of the Letter and the City

When I go hiking, I carefully study topographical maps to understand the direction, length, and challenges of the trail ahead. I usually have the AllTrails map downloaded on my phone. The map provides a sense of security and orientation, enabling me to track my progress and anticipate what lies ahead. Without it, the trek would feel uncertain and disorienting to me. In much the same way, the purpose of the following section is to offer a broad, guiding map for navigating the content and context of 1 Corinthians.

Just as a map notes key landmarks to keep the traveler on course, this overview focuses on the significant themes and developments in Paul's letter to help you navigate its complexities. While not exhaustive, it nonetheless provides a structured framework that clarifies Paul's message and addresses the pressing issues within the Corinthian community. By following these thematic landmarks, you'll be better equipped to anticipate and understand the pivotal moments of the letter as they unfold—just like a well-prepared hiker uses a map to anticipate the challenges of the terrain.

Below is a general summary of the content and flow of 1 Corinthians, designed to guide you through its major themes and issues. After examining the letter's content, we'll turn to a broader survey of the city of Corinth and its population.

An Overview of the Contents of 1 Corinthians

The Opening Section

The first theme appears in the opening section (1:1-9), where Paul addresses his letter to "the church (ἐκκλησία) of God that is in Corinth." The term ἐκκλησία is a crucial concept in 1 Corinthians, appearing twenty-two times. Scholars have widely debated the term's origin. While the modern English term "church" typically refers to a religious assembly, and has little to no use outside religious contexts, in the ancient Greek world the Greek word ἐκκλησία was commonly used to refer to a public assembly or gathering within a polis (e.g., see Acts 19:32, 39, 41). The primary purpose of such public gatherings was "to make a range of decisions affecting their common life" (Trebilco 2011: 165), underscoring its political connotations. For Paul, however, the assembly to whom he is addressing his letter is no ordinary gathering: it consists of those who have been sanctified (ἡγιασμένοις), that is, the saints (ἁγίοις). Furthermore, Paul's tone in this opening section is calm and positive. He gives thanks to God for the ways in which the Corinthians have been enriched in all speech and knowledge (ἐν παντὶ λόγῳ καὶ πάσῃ γνώσει) and for lacking no spiritual gifts (χαρίσματα).

Response to an Indirect Source

In 1 Corinthians 1:10–6:20, Paul addresses troubling news he has received from Chloe's people about the Corinthians (1:11). The issue seems to center on their rejection of Paul's authority and leadership. As a result, this section focuses primarily on Paul's defense of his authority over the community, and this establishes the tone for the entire letter. Paul expresses his displeasure upon hearing that some Corinthians have turned away from him and aligned themselves with other leaders. He acknowledges that his message of the cross may seem foolish or a stumbling block to some, but he asserts that it is, in fact, the wisdom of God. Thus, the themes of speech (*logos*) and wisdom (*sophia*) are central to chapters 1 and 2.

In chapters 3 and 4, Paul continues to address the divisions and the rejection of his authority. He portrays himself in various roles, including as a mother, planter, builder, and father, emphasizing the significance and breadth of his work in the Corinthian community. He warns the Corinthians not to underestimate him. After describing himself as their father and urging them to imitate him (4:15-16), Paul calls out certain individuals (τινες) in Corinth who claim he will not return. He accuses these people of arrogance, asserting that when he does come, he wants to see their power, not just their words. Paul even threatens to come with a rod of discipline.

Not content with that, Paul then turns to another report that he has heard about the Corinthians: about *pornea* (chapter 5). According to the report, some guy has his father's wife. What exactly does this mean? Although it is often translated as "sexual immorality," the exact meaning of this Greek term is highly debated in scholarship, as we will see later. Again, Paul is not happy with the way the Corinthians acted toward this man (5:2). He makes it clear that they must remove him from their community (5:5-7, 13). Then, from chapter 5 to chapter 6, there is a sudden break in topic, resulting in Paul suddenly switching to a discussion on how to handle grievance in the community. He forbids the Corinthians from taking such cases "to court before the unrighteous." (6:1). Why? Paul's reason is very simple: because it is the righteous who will judge the world (6:2). In other words, he wants the conflicts to be resolved internally. The issue of *porneia* and body then returns in 6:12-20.

Response to a Direct Source

This section begins in chapter 7, where we find the first occurrence of περὶ δέ (often translated as "now concerning"), probably indicating that Paul is addressing specific questions that the Corinthians asked of him. The first topic in this section revolves around marriage (7:1-24), focusing primarily on issues related to sexuality. The Corinthians ask about the statement, "It is well for a man not to touch a woman" (7:1), essentially raising the question of whether complete abstinence is the ideal way to live. Paul provides a nuanced response. For married couples, he asserts that both the wife and the husband have authority over each other's bodies, emphasizing mutual responsibility. He advises that they should not deprive one another, except by mutual agreement and only for a limited time (7:5).

As for the unmarried (τοῖς ἀγάμοις), Paul encourages them to remain unmarried, as he is (7:8). However, he acknowledges that if they cannot exercise self-control, it is better for them to marry than to burn with passion. Paul also addresses the issue of divorce. He instructs the Corinthians that if someone is married to an unbeliever, they should remain married. However, if the unbeliever chooses to leave, the believer should allow it (7:12-15). Paul's overarching principle is that one should remain in the condition in which they were called. "This is my rule in all the churches," he insists. Whether married, unmarried, circumcised, uncircumcised, enslaved, or free, Paul advises believers to stay as they are. Notably, when speaking to slaves, Paul emphasizes that although they may be enslaved in the present, in the Lord they are spiritually free. He reminds them that Christ has bought them with a price, underscoring the idea that their true identity and freedom are found in Christ, not in their social status.

The *second* theme Paul addresses is related to virgins (τῶν παρθένων), or unmarried people. Here, Paul continues to encourage individuals to remain as they are. While he does not forbid marriage, he seems to caution that it brings difficulties. He states, "Those who marry will experience distress in this life, and I would spare you that" (7:28). Paul's reasoning is rooted in his apocalyptic worldview: he believes the end is near. Therefore, he advises, "from now on, let those who have wives be as though they had none" (7:29). Why? Because, as he explains, "the present form of this world is passing away" (7:31). Paul's eschatological vision shapes his counsel on social issues, urging the Corinthians to focus on the impending transformation of the world rather than on earthly attachments like marriage.

The *third* theme in chapter 8 addresses the issue of food sacrificed to idols. Paul is concerned about certain members of the community who claim to possess particular knowledge, arguing that since idols are not real and there is only one true God (8:4), it is permissible to eat food offered to idols. However, Paul emphasizes that not everyone shares this understanding. Some believers, whose consciences are weaker, may feel defiled when they eat such food because they still associate it with idol worship (8:7). Paul's key point appears in verses 8-9: "We are no worse off if we do not eat, and no better off if we do. But take care that this liberty of yours does not somehow become a stumbling block to the weak." While Paul acknowledges the freedom believers have in Christ, he cautions that this freedom must be exercised responsibly, not harming or misleading those with weaker consciences.

Precipitously, Paul then launches into a robust defense of his apostleship, using rhetorical questions to affirm his authority: "Am I not free? Am I not an apostle? Have I not seen Jesus our Lord? Are you not my work in the Lord?" (9:1). He asserts his right to receive material support for his ministry, drawing from everyday examples like soldiers being paid and farmers benefiting from their crops to argue that those who preach the gospel should be supported (9:14). However, Paul explains that he voluntarily chooses not to claim this right, preferring to preach the gospel free of charge to avoid accusations of personal gain (9:15-18). He also highlights his adaptability, becoming "like a Jew" to win Jews, "like one under the law" to reach those under the law, and "like one without the law" to reach Gentiles. Paul concludes by comparing his life to a race, emphasizing self-discipline and focus as essential elements of his ministry.

In chapter 10, Paul shifts to recount the story of Moses and the Israelites passing through the sea under a cloud, interpreting it as a symbol of baptism (10:2). Despite all the Israelites experiencing the same spiritual blessings, some were struck down by God for their disobedience. Paul warns the Corinthians that participating in the same community and sacraments does not guarantee divine favor. He connects idolatry with sexual immorality, citing instances in which the Israelites fell into sin and were punished. He further warns against idol worship, equating food offered to idols with food sacrificed to demons, declaring, "You cannot drink the cup of the Lord and the cup of demons" (10:21). This abrupt shift may understandably have confused the Corinthians, for though Paul initially argued that idols are nothing, he now warns the Corinthians of the danger associated with eating such food.

Despite his strong stance, Paul returns to a more moderate tone, repeating his principle: "All things are lawful, but not all things are beneficial. All things are lawful, but not all things build up" (10:23). While some scholars speculate that the phrase "all things are lawful" was a Corinthian slogan, Paul's struggle to balance his arguments suggests a tension in his own reasoning. He advises that if unbelievers invite believers to eat, believers may eat whatever is offered to them. However, if someone objects that the food has been sacrificed to idols, the Corinthian believers should refrain from eating *out of consideration for others* (10:27-30). In this, Paul strives to maintain both theological consistency and practical guidance for communal harmony.

The *fourth* theme, in 11:2-16, addresses gender hierarchy and proper conduct in worship. Paul begins by praising the Corinthians for remembering his teachings, but he quickly moves to outline a hierarchical structure: Christ is the head of every man, man is the head of a woman, and God is the head of Christ. Based on this structure, Paul argues that men should not cover their heads while praying or prophesying, as they are the "image and reflection of God," while women should cover their heads as a sign of submission, being the "reflection of man" (11:8). For Paul, the head covering serves as a sign that a woman is under an authority (11:10), reflecting the gender roles established by the created order.

The *fifth* theme, in 11:17-33, concerns the Lord's Supper. Here Paul expresses anger over reports of improper behavior during communal meals. He criticizes the Corinthians for ostensibly gathering as a church (*ekklesia*) but treating that gathering as an occasion to eat their own food, leading to a division between the wealthy, who eat and drink to excess, and the poor, who go hungry (11:18-21). This behavior humiliates those who have less, and Paul condemns it as unworthy of the Lord's Supper. He reminds the Corinthians of the sacred nature of the meal, urging them to discern the body of Christ when partaking of the bread and cup. Paul warns that failure to do so has led to sickness and even death among some of them.

The *sixth* theme is on spiritual people or things (τῶν πνευματικῶν). This section can be divided into three subsections. First, Paul's acknowledgment of the presence of multiple gifts, services, and activities (12:4-6) in the church of Corinth—with a warning that a person should not use their gift to curse Jesus. In order to illustrate the importance of these activities or gifts in a community, Paul uses the analogy of a body (12:12-26), demonstrating that each part of the body is as important and necessary as the others. After he discusses the body analogy, he presents a famous treatise on love in chapter 13. In chapter 14, Paul focuses on two gifts: tongue(s) and prophecy. The core of his argument rests on the idea that the public use of foreign languages is useless and therefore needs to be accompanied by translation. Prophecy is more important than tongues because it uses words that are understandable. If foreign languages are present without translation, for Paul it is better for them not to be spoken.

The *seventh* theme in chapter 15 has to do with the doctrine of the resurrection. While chapters 1 and 2 focused on Paul's preaching of the cross, in this penultimate section Paul highlights that his gospel (15:1) is not only about the cross but also centers on the resurrection of

Christ. Some Corinthians were challenging the notion of the resurrection, claiming that there is no resurrection of the dead (15:12), which would imply that Christ remained dead in the grave. Paul counters this by arguing that "if Christ has not been raised, then our proclamation has been in vain and your faith has been in vain" (15:14). For Paul, both the cross and the resurrection are inseparable parts of the gospel (15:3-4). He reinforces his argument by pointing to the numerous witnesses who saw the resurrected Christ, including over five hundred people, many of whom were still alive at the time of writing (15:5-11). This, Paul contends, is evidence that the resurrection is not only a theological doctrine but also a verifiable historical event. Moreover, Christ's resurrection is central to the Christian faith because it guarantees a future resurrection for believers. Paul describes Christ as "the first fruits" of the resurrection, underscoring that through Christ's victory over death, the final enemy—death itself—will eventually be destroyed, and all will be subjected to God, who will be "all in all" (15:28).

After laying out the importance of the resurrection, Paul addresses its practical implications, particularly regarding the practice of baptism for the dead. He argues that if there is no resurrection, then this practice is meaningless (15:29). The idea of baptism for the dead has generated much scholarly debate, for it seems perplexing from a Western worldview that views death as final. However, in the first-century Corinthian context, this practice may have been common (DeMaris 1995). As Paul often does, he shifts to boasting about his sufferings for Christ (15:30-34), stressing that if there is no resurrection, his suffering would be pointless. Paul then responds to a skeptic's question about how the dead are raised and with what kind of body. He begins sharply, calling the questioner a "fool!" He uses the analogy of a seed that must die before it can come to life, explaining that the resurrected body will be fundamentally different from the current physical body. "What is sown is perishable; what is raised is imperishable ... It is sown in weakness; it is raised in power" (15:42-44). For Paul, the resurrection brings about a radical transformation because "flesh and blood cannot inherit the kingdom of God," and all will be changed in an instant (15:50-52).

The *eighth* theme, introduced in 16:1-4, focuses on the practical matter of financial contributions. There is an Indonesian saying, "*ujung-ujungnya duit*" (meaning "in the end, it all comes down to money"), which reflects how, after all of Paul's theological arguments, the conversation climaxes with the discussion about the collection. Paul instructs the Corinthians to set aside part of their earnings on the first day of every week, just as he had directed the churches in Galatia. These contributions are to be collected regularly so that, when he arrives, the funds are ready and can be sent to the believers in Jerusalem. Paul even suggests that he might accompany the person delivering the gift.

The Closing Section

In the closing section of the letter, Paul promises the Corinthians that he will come back again to visit them on his way to Macedonia. He wants to spend the winter season with them. He then makes sure that when Timothy comes to Corinth, they will treat him well. He explains that he tried to encourage Apollos to visit them, but for whatever reason Apollos refuses to do so. The letter then ends with some words of encouragement and greetings.

The City of Corinth

The city of Corinth during Paul's time was a bustling, cosmopolitan hub strategically located at the crossroads of important trade routes. Situated on the Isthmus of Corinth, a narrow land bridge that connected northern and southern Greece, Corinth became a vital center for commerce, linking the Aegean Sea to the east and the Adriatic Sea to the west. Two major ports, Lechaeum and Cenchreae, facilitated the easy exchange of goods between Asia and Italy, further amplifying Corinth's significance in the ancient Mediterranean economy. Strabo, a first-century CE geographer, emphasizes Corinth's wealth due to its strategic position and commerce, stating, "Corinth is called 'wealthy' because of its commerce, since it is situated on the Isthmus and is master of two harbors, of which one leads straight to Asia, and the other to Italy; and it makes easy the exchange of merchandise from both countries that are so far distant from each other" (*Geography* 8.6.20).

Before Roman dominance, Corinth had already been an influential city-state in Greece, known for its commercial activity and strategic position. Pausanias, a Greek geographer, recorded a local tradition—that Corinth was named after Corinthus, a son of Zeus, although this was acknowledged as more myth than historical fact (*Description of Greece* 2.1.1). Corinth's prosperity is further reflected in the widespread distribution of Corinthian pottery throughout the Mediterranean, particularly in the western Mediterranean (Naerebout and Singor 2014: 96). Excavations confirm that Corinth remained a center of trade from the Early to Late Helladic periods. Carl W. Blegen underscores this continuity: "The prosperity of this region was no doubt largely due to commerce. The results of the excavations ... make it clear that Early, Middle, and Late Helladic Periods alike, Corinth was consistently a center of trade" (Blegen 1920: 8).

This prominence gave Corinth a unique identity, distinct from cultural or religious centers like Athens, Delphi, or Olympia. As Mary Roebuck notes, "Corinth cannot be equated with sanctuaries like Delphi and Olympia, nor with a city such as Athens. Corinth was essentially an industrial city" (Roebuck 1990: 47, 1972). Its geographical advantage of proximity to two major harbor towns—Lechaeum and Kenchreai—connecting the Saronic and Corinthian gulfs "gave Corinth its real importance" (Tomlinson 1992: 75).

Corinth's economy was further enriched by the presence of the *diolkos*, a paved road across the narrowest section of the Isthmus, connecting the Saronic and Corinthian gulfs. While the exact function of the *diolkos* has been debated among scholars, its contribution to the Corinthian economy was undeniable, even into the Roman period. David Pettegrew explains, "Merchants benefited by this shortcut in long-distance trade, while Corinth received revenues on the tolls, transport fees, and services to passengers in transit" (Pettegrew 2016: 158).

In addition to its geographical and economic significance, Corinth's religious life was vibrant. The city was home to temples dedicated to Apollo, Aphrodite (built around the fifth century BCE), Asclepius (built around the fourth century BCE), and Poseidon at Isthmus (built around the eighth century BCE). The Temple of Aphrodite was particularly prominent in pre-Roman Corinth, with Strabo describing it as "so rich that it owned more than a thousand temple-slaves, prostitutes, whom both men and women had dedicated to the goddess" (*Geography* 8.6.20c). The presence of such religious structures attracted visitors from many places, further solidifying Corinth's role as a significant cultural and religious center in the ancient world.

A Destroyed and Colonized City

In 146 BCE, Corinth faced a significant turning point when Roman forces, under Lucius Mummius, destroyed the city during the Roman conquest of Greece. Corinth was razed, its population either enslaved or killed, and its wealth plundered. The severity of Corinth's depopulation after its destruction has been a subject of scholarly debate. Most scholars, however, agree that the city was not entirely depopulated. Cicero's testimony suggests that the land remained inhabited despite the ruin. While the Romans likely deported the upper class, Corinth was repopulated with a new aristocracy in 44 BCE. This continuity between Hellenistic and Roman Corinth is crucial to understanding the city's development. David Gilman Romano notes, "there was continuous occupation in Corinth between 146–44 BC for farming and grazing activities, and numerous agricultural interests may have existed in the area." (Romano 1994: 13) However, despite the remnants of the old city, significant political activity in Corinth during this period was unlikely, as evidenced by the absence of coin minting in the interregnum. As Romano writes, "[T]he Greek city was deprived of its civic and political identity" (Romano 2005: 585). During this time, Corinth was an "almost-deserted ghost town" (Sanders 2005: 22).

Julius Caesar's transformation of Corinth into a Roman colony marked a significant shift in the city's identity. During the Flavian period, particularly under Vespasian's reign, the city's name changed again to *Colonia Iulia Flavia Augusta Corinthiensis*. The Roman restructuring of Corinth encompassed both the reuse of key Hellenistic structures—such as the theater, the South Stoa, and the Archaic Temple—and the construction of new Roman buildings, including the Forum, and this particular structure became the focal point for social, economic, and governmental activities. The blending of Hellenistic and Roman elements highlights both the practical reuse of existing structures and the broader Roman strategy of asserting dominance while maintaining a degree of continuity with the past.

In the Roman era, Corinth regained its prominence as a wealthy commercial city on the Peloponnesian peninsula, but it was now a colonized city under Roman rule. On the surface, the city appeared prosperous, with grand Roman buildings reflecting its wealth and status. However, beneath this splendor lay the remnants of the old city, silent witnesses to the brutality of the Roman conquest. As Walbank explains, "[I]n Roman eyes *Colonia Laus Iulia Corinthiensis* was an entirely new foundation. Greek Corinth had ceased to exist with the destruction of its political functions and civic buildings; although approximately the same site was used, the Romans were founding a new city, not rehabilitating an old one" (Walbank 1997: 107). This duality—Roman prosperity built on the ruins of Greek Corinth—represents the deeper narrative of cultural erasure and displacement that characterized the city's transformation under Roman rule (see Engels 1990: 16–21; Romano 2003: 293–8; Bookidis 2005; Robinson 2005: 101–40; Pawlak 2014). While commerce and wealth flourished, Corinth's Hellenistic identity had been effectively erased, leaving behind a city that bore the scars of its violent past.

In the process of rebuilding Corinth, it is commonly known that Julius Caesar sent two primary groups of people—veterans and freedpersons—to inhabit the city. However, both literary evidence and onomastic studies suggest that the number of veterans was significantly smaller than that of freedpersons in Roman Corinth. This supports Strabo's statement that "now after Corinth had remained deserted for a long time, it was restored again, because of its favorable position, by the deified Caesar, who colonized it with people that belonged for the most part to the freedmen class" (*Geography* 8.6.23). Spawforth's prosopographic study of names found in duoviral coinage and epigraphy of Roman Corinth demonstrates that many of these freedpersons were "Greeks returning home" and that they occupied elite positions in society (Spawforth 1996: 175).

Benjamin Millis expands on Spawforth's thesis by arguing that these Corinthian freedpersons were not Romanized Greeks, but "entirely Greek in origin." Millis emphasizes that these individuals represented "a very special group of people" capable of navigating the cultural interconnectedness between Roman and Greek identities. He writes:

> It was not one which had so thoroughly identified itself with Roman culture as to lose its facility for Greek language and culture, but neither was it an immigrant group in the process of assimilation which had acquired merely a veneer of Romanness while remaining essentially Greek. Instead, it was a hybrid of both cultures—a group in which one language became the mode of expression within the public sphere and another within the private.
>
> (Millis 2010: 31)

Despite the multilingual nature of the eastern Mediterranean from which many of these freedpersons originated, Greek remained the dominant language in the region. However, it is likely that Greek was not the only language they spoke. The social and linguistic landscape of Roman Corinth was thus far more complex than the simple binary of Greek and Latin often employed in scholarly analyses. The presence of multiple languages suggests that Corinth's sociolinguistic environment was shaped by a dynamic interplay between Roman and Greek influences, where public and private expressions of identity could shift fluidly between these cultural spheres (Tupamahu 2022).

Given all this information, it thus becomes clearer that the Corinthians were not simply a community shaped by Roman colonization but were also marked by the complex interplay of cultural, linguistic, and social forces. This layered identity of Corinth as a hybrid and cosmopolitan city provides vital context for understanding the social dynamics that influenced Paul's ministry and the challenges faced by the early Christian church in Corinth. Thus, to understand Roman Corinth during Paul's time, it is helpful to view the city as a bustling economic center, comparable to modern-day New York City in its diversity, energy, and significance for trade and cultural exchange. Yet beneath this thriving exterior lay a history of destruction, colonization, and cultural erasure, which we will come to a bit later.

The Corinthians

What do we know about the Corinthians from Paul's discourses about them in 1 Corinthians?

1 *That They Were a Diverse Population:* Corinth's population during Paul's time was composed of individuals from various parts of the Mediterranean, including Roman settlers, freed slaves, veterans, and local Greeks. This diversity contributed to the city's dynamic social fabric and its reputation as a melting pot of cultures and economic opportunity.

2. *That They Had Experienced Both Trauma and Rebuilding:* The people of Corinth had experienced collective trauma due to the city's destruction in 146 BCE. Both the survivors and the new settlers brought in under Roman rule bore the psychological and cultural marks of this traumatic history. The destruction and subsequent rebuilding under Roman control profoundly shaped the city's identity and the attitudes of its inhabitants toward power, community, and social status.

3. *That This Roman Colony Was Heavily Influenced by Roman Imperial Rule:* The city's architecture, social structures, and economy reflected broader Roman imperial realities. The struggle for social and economic status in this cosmopolitan setting deeply affected daily life in Corinth, shaping the ways in which people engaged with the city's institutions, including religious and social organizations.

4. *That Corinthians Were Marked by Religious Pluralism:* Corinth's religious life was shaped by a blend of Greek and Roman practices, with temples dedicated to gods such as Apollo, Aphrodite, Asclepius, and Poseidon. The religious plurality of the city contributed to its reputation as a cosmopolitan hub and shaped the religious environment in which early Christian communities like Paul's congregation interacted.

5. *That They Experienced Substantial Economic Inequality:* Despite the city's wealth, there was significant economic disparity between different social classes. Freed slaves, lower-class laborers, and veterans coexisted with wealthy aristocrats, creating tensions around wealth, status, and privilege. This inequality is reflected in Paul's letters to the Corinthians, where he addresses issues of division, social hierarchies, and the treatment of the poor within the Christian community.

6. *That They Had a Hybrid Identity:* The freedpersons who populated Corinth were not merely Roman or Greek but represented a unique hybrid identity. They were able to navigate the dual worlds of Roman political and social expectations while maintaining their Greek cultural roots. This hybridity influenced how the Corinthians perceived themselves in relation to Rome and other Greek cities.

7. *That They Were Multilingual:* The population of Corinth was likely multilingual, with Greek as the dominant language. However, given Corinth's status as a major commercial hub and the diversity of its inhabitants, it is probable that other languages, such as Latin, were spoken in both public and private contexts. The complexity of Corinth's linguistic environment is crucial for understanding the cultural and social dynamics within the city.

8   *That They Were Culturally Fluid:* The Corinthians, particularly the elite freedpersons, were adept at balancing Roman and Greek cultural elements. This fluidity allowed them to participate in Roman civic life while still retaining their Greek heritage. This hybridity would have created both tensions and opportunities for the early Christian community as they sought to form their identity in a city deeply embedded in two cultural worlds.

9   *That They Experienced Economic and Social Tensions:* The presence of freedpersons in elite social positions may have created economic and social tensions within the city, particularly between different groups vying for status and influence. Paul's letters, which address tensions within the Corinthian church, reflect these broader social tensions, highlighting issues of status, wealth, and power that were prevalent in Corinthian society.

These observations provide essential contextual clues for understanding Paul's relationship with the Corinthian church. The city's complex social fabric, history of trauma, and Roman imperial influence all contributed to the dynamics that Paul addressed in his letters. Corinth, as a microcosm of the broader Roman world, represented both the opportunities and the challenges that early Christian communities faced as they navigated life in a diverse, cosmopolitan, and colonized city. The city's inhabitants were not merely a monolithic group of Roman colonists or Hellenistic Greeks, but a hybrid population that embodied elements of both Greekness and Romanness. These dynamics would have shaped how Paul's message was received, understood, and applied by the diverse Corinthian church. As a cosmopolitan city with complex social, economic, and linguistic realities, Corinth presented unique challenges and opportunities for the early Christian community, which had to navigate these various influences in its practice of faith. The letter of first Corinthians reveals the messiness of early followers of Jesus, where issues of power, identity, and belonging were constantly negotiated.

In Closing

Just as a hiker relies on a map to navigate unfamiliar terrain, understanding the content of Paul's letter and the context of Corinth gives us the necessary orientation for interpreting 1 Corinthians. Corinth's complex social, economic, and cultural landscape, much like a challenging trail, shaped the dynamics of the early Christian community. By mapping out these key themes, we can now confidently move forward, equipped to navigate the twists and turns of Paul's responses to the pressing issues faced by the Corinthians. With this overview in hand, we are ready to explore the more intricate details of the journey ahead.

3

Paul and the Corinthian Defiance

Mentions of "Corinth" and "Corinthians" are relatively scarce in the New Testament, appearing only twice in Acts (18:1; 19:1), once in 1 Corinthians (1:2), twice in 2 Corinthians (1:1, 23), and once in 2 Timothy (4:20). Beyond 1 and 2 Corinthians, the book of Acts provides the primary source for understanding Paul's relationship with the Corinthian church. In this chapter, we will explore how Paul's relationship with the Corinthians is depicted in Acts, and how Paul himself reflects on this relationship in his correspondence with the Corinthian community, particularly in 1 Corinthians. This relationship is crucial for understanding the larger dynamics of the letter, as one cannot fully interpret 1 Corinthians without accounting for the interpersonal and authoritative tensions that underlie Paul's dealings with this community.

The Description of Acts

Since the nineteenth century, scholars have raised significant questions about the historicity of Acts, beginning with F. C. Baur, who famously critiqued the book as overly sympathetic to Paul. Baur argued that Acts demonstrates a clear tendency (*Tendenz*) to defend Paul's ministry, positioning him in an overly favorable light, thus compromising the historical accuracy of the narrative (Baur 1873: 5–14). In this view, Acts is not a neutral account but one shaped by the agenda of a "Paulinist" writer who sought to portray Paul as the uncontested leader of early Christianity. This leads to the suspicion that Acts cannot be relied upon as an objective historical document. More recent scholars have nuanced Baur's critique by considering Acts within the genre of "apologetic historiography," a form of writing not strictly aimed at factual accuracy but at shaping the identity and self-perception of a community (Sterling 1992, 2023; Kee 1997; Penner 2004; Adams 2012). Despite these concerns, Acts remains a crucial text for reconstructing Paul's ministry, particularly because it is the only extended source outside of

Paul's own letters that offers a narrative of his activities, including of his time in Corinth.

According to Acts, Paul's relationship with the Corinthians begins during his first recorded journey to Greece (Acts 17–18). The text is ambiguous as to whether this was Paul's first visit to Greece or not, but the narrative itself does not speak about any previous encounters between Paul and the Corinthians. The sequence begins with a vision Paul receives at night, in which a figure from Macedonia implores him to come and offer help. Immediately following this vision, Paul travels to Philippi, passing through Samothrace and Neapolis before proceeding to Thessalonica, Beroea, and finally Athens. In Athens, Paul engages in a theological dispute with Greek philosophers at the Areopagus, highlighting the cultural and intellectual contrasts between his monotheistic message and the prevailing Greek philosophies. From Athens, Paul makes his way to Corinth, a bustling port city known for its commercial wealth, diverse population, and reputation for moral licentiousness. This, it appears, is Paul's first substantial interaction with the Corinthian community.

Upon arriving in Corinth, Paul meets a Jewish couple, Priscilla and Aquila, who had been expelled from Rome under the decree of Emperor Claudius. Acts 18:2 notes that Claudius ordered the expulsion of Jews from Rome, likely as a measure to quell unrest within the Jewish community, as Leonard Rutgers suggests (Rutgers 1994: 65–6). As it did many others, this decree displaced Priscilla and Aquila, and they ended up in Corinth, where they encountered Paul. Although Aquila is explicitly identified as Jewish, the text does not clarify whether Priscilla shares this identity, though the fact that they both have Latin names suggests that they, like many Jews in the diaspora, adopted Greek or Roman names for cultural and practical reasons. It is also worth noting that Paul's own name (*Paullus*) is a Latin name, meaning "small," perhaps reflecting a broader tendency among Jews in the diaspora to navigate their hybrid identities by adopting names from dominant cultures.

Paul's letters give evidence of Priscilla and Aquila's significance in early Christian circles, mentioning them as important figures. At the conclusion of 1 Corinthians, Paul writes, "Aquila and Prisca, together with the church in their house, greet you warmly in the Lord" (1 Cor. 16:19). Interestingly, while Acts refers to them as "Priscilla and Aquila," Paul in 1 Corinthians reverses the order to "Aquila and Prisca," and further, uses the more formal version of her name, "Prisca." This difference in naming conventions has intrigued scholars, some of whom argue that the diminutive "Priscilla" in Acts may reflect a scribal tendency to diminish the role of women in early Christianity. Dominika Kurek-Chomycz, for example, argues that the diminutive form could be part of an "anti-women" agenda in certain scribal traditions, aimed at devaluing her authority (Kurek-Chomycz 2006; see also Fellows 2022). Regardless of these textual variations and their possible significance, it is clear that Prisca (or Priscilla) was a key leader in the early Christian movement in Corinth.

In addition to being prominent leaders, Priscilla and Aquila were also tentmakers, a trade they shared with Paul (Acts 18:3). Paul's involvement in tentmaking reflects his position as a "non-literary artisan," a common status for many itinerant preachers and workers in the Roman Empire. Adolf Deissmann characterizes Paul as a man who earned his living through physical labor, rather than through intellectual or literary pursuits, grounding his social existence in the economic realities of working-class life (Deissmann 1957: 51). This aspect of Paul's life is particularly significant because it situates him within the economic and social strata of the communities he evangelized. Acts suggests that when Silas and Timothy arrived in Corinth, Paul found more time to focus on his preaching, possibly because they took on some of the financial burdens for him (Acts 18:5).

The reference to the "church in their house" (1 Cor. 16:19) indicates that Priscilla and Aquila were not just economic partners but also played a critical role in the establishment of the early Christian community in Corinth. That they correct Apollos, an eloquent teacher from Alexandria, whose knowledge of "the Way of God" they deemed incomplete (Acts 18:26), further demonstrates their authority. They seem to have wielded considerable influence in shaping the theological direction of the early church, a role that Paul affirms when he refers to them as his co-workers in Romans 16:3. Although the text does not tell us how long Priscilla and Aquila remained in Corinth, Acts later mentions that they traveled with Paul to Ephesus and Syria, reinforcing their close collaboration with him (Acts 18:18, 26).

The central focus of Acts 18, however, is Paul's conflict with the Jewish community in Corinth. Paul initially directs his message toward the Jews, preaching in the synagogue every Sabbath and attempting to convince both Jews and Greeks that "the Messiah was Jesus" (Acts 18:5). His message, however, meets with resistance from the Jewish community, prompting Paul to turn his focus to the Gentiles (Acts 18:6). Despite the opposition, Paul manages to gain several prominent converts, including Crispus, the synagogue official (ὁ ἀρχισυνάγωγος), who becomes a follower of Jesus. According to Acts, most of the opposition Paul faced in Corinth came from the Jewish community, opposition which seems to set the stage for the later conflict between Paul and the wider Jewish world.

One of the more puzzling episodes in Acts is the account of the Jewish community bringing Paul before Gallio, the Roman proconsul in Achaia, accusing him of persuading people to worship God in ways contrary to Jewish law. Gallio, clearly indifferent to intra-Jewish disputes, dismisses the case, stating that it falls outside his jurisdiction (Acts 18:12-16). After Gallio's refusal to intervene, the Jews seize Sosthenes, another synagogue official, and beat him in front of the tribunal (Acts 18:17). This sudden act of violence is striking, not only for its brutality but also for the anti-Jewish undertones it conveys. Acts does not provide any background on Sosthenes, and his abrupt entrance into the narrative has prompted some scholars, like Chrysostom, to speculate that Sosthenes and Crispus might be the same person (*Homilies on Acts* 39.1–2; cf. Myrou 1999). Whether they are indeed the same person remains unclear, but the lack of clarity certainly adds to the tension of the narrative.

Acts recounts that in addition to Crispus, "many of the Corinthians who heard Paul became believers and were baptized" (Acts 18:8). The text does not specify the exact number of converts, and Paul himself provides a somewhat contradictory account in 1 Corinthians, where he claims to have baptized no one in Corinth except Crispus and Gaius—though he later corrects himself by adding that he also baptized the household of Stephanas (1 Cor. 1:14, 16). This growth in believers represents the founding of the Corinthian assembly, a community that would later present significant challenges to Paul's authority.

One of the more curious aspects of Acts is its silence on Paul's letters to the Corinthians. Given that Acts was written long after 1 and 2 Corinthians, the absence of any reference to these letters is striking. Scholars have long debated whether the author of Acts was even aware of Paul's letters, with some suggesting that the silence reflects a deliberate decision to downplay Paul's epistolary legacy (Enslin 1938, 1970; Knox 1966; Goulder 1986; Adams 2012; Tupamahu 2022). The lack of mention is even more puzzling in light of Paul's own silence on the violent confrontation with the Jews before Gallio or the beating of Sosthenes. If these incidents were as significant as Acts portrays them to be, then it is curious that Paul makes no mention of them in his letters, especially in 1 and 2 Corinthians, which deal extensively with his relationship with the Corinthian community. This silence may hint at deeper complexities in Paul's relationship with the Corinthians, which Acts chooses not to address.

Moreover, Acts does not provide any account of the internal conflicts within the Corinthian church that Paul discusses in his letters. Instead, it focuses on the conflict between Paul and the Jewish community. After Paul's departure from Corinth, Apollos, a Jewish follower of Jesus from Alexandria, enters the scene. Described as an eloquent speaker and knowledgeable in the Scriptures, Apollos quickly gains a following (Acts 18:24). Acts does not indicate whether Paul knew or interacted with Apollos, but it does not present any conflict between the two figures. Priscilla and Aquila correct some aspects of Apollos's teaching, though Acts earlier states that he taught "accurately [ἀκριβῶς] the things concerning Jesus" (Acts 18:25). This raises the question of what exactly Priscilla and Aquila found lacking in Apollos's message, a detail Acts does not clarify. After receiving their instruction, Apollos travels to Achaia, likely to Corinth, where he preaches the same message as Paul: that "the Messiah is Jesus" (Acts 18:28).

In 1 Corinthians, however, Apollos's name appears seven times (1 Cor. 1:12; 3:4, 5, 6, 22; 6:12), indicating that Paul was aware of his presence in Corinth, though it remains unclear whether they ever met. Some scholars have argued that Apollos may have been one of the catalysts for division within the Corinthian church, as his eloquent style and theological depth attracted a significant following that may have rivaled Paul's influence (Horsley 1977: 231–2; Brown 1997: 151). The division between the "followers of Paul and Apollos" is one of the central concerns in 1 Corinthians (Wire 1990: 161), though Acts is entirely silent on this issue. Whether Apollos contributed to the tensions in Corinth remains unclear from the Acts narrative, leaving room for further speculation on the dynamics between Paul, Apollos, and the Corinthian community.

The Description of 1 Corinthians

I mentioned in the first chapter of this book that our knowledge of the Corinthian church comes primarily from Paul himself, apart from what is recorded in the book of Acts. More significantly, 1 Corinthians was written largely in response to a report Paul received about the state of the church. After the conventional opening of his letter—which includes the sender's name, the recipients, a prayer, and thanksgiving—Paul abruptly transitions into an expression of his disappointment, lamenting that "it has been reported to me by Chloe's people that there are quarrels among you" (1 Cor. 1:11). Chloe's people (τῶν Χλόης) delivered a concerning report about the Corinthians, and Paul took this report seriously. Who exactly are Chloe's people? We know very little about them, as this is the only reference to them in the entire New Testament. What might Chloe's people have hoped to achieve by reporting these divisions to Paul? Were they acting out of loyalty to him, or were they trying to influence the power dynamics within the community?

Many scholars have speculated that they may have been enslaved persons or freedpersons, since the genitive construction in Greek could indicate that they *belonged* to Chloe (Welborn 1987; Fee 1988; Meeks 2003; Friesen 2004; Theissen 2004; Horsley 2011; Nasrallah 2014; Smith 2023). This is plausible; if they had been Chloe's children, they would likely be identified by their father's name rather than their mother's, as Theissen points out (Theissen 2004; Thiselton 2013). Chloe was therefore likely a slave owner or a patron of some influence in Corinth.

Paul's letter of rebuke, then, was based on this report, which was more than mere gossip but seems to have reflected deep concerns about the church's internal dynamics. While we don't know Chloe's motivations or why her people reported the divisions to Paul, it is evident that Paul was displeased. In fact, his dissatisfaction is so intense that he even threatens to come to Corinth with a stick, suggesting physical discipline (1 Cor. 4:21). Paul devotes the first six chapters of 1 Corinthians to addressing the issues he learned from Chloe's people before turning in chapter 7 to the questions the Corinthians themselves had sent him (1 Cor. 7:1).

Paul's concern is not only with the divisions (σχίσματα) within the community, but also with the quarrels (ἔριδες) and jealousy (ζῆλος) that have taken root among them (1 Cor. 1:11, 3:3). According to the report, different factions in Corinth claim allegiance to various leaders: some say they follow Paul, others Apollos, others Cephas (Peter), and still others claim to follow Christ directly (1 Cor. 1:12). Paul perceives these divisions as a serious threat to the church's unity and well-being. What, more precisely, was the nature of these "divisions"?

Are the Corinthians Really Divided?

A reading of 1 Corinthians 1–4 might suggest that the church in Corinth was deeply divided, with its members engaged in intense rivalries. Richard Horsley, for example, contends that Paul wrote this letter specifically to address the issue of divisions that had arisen within the newly established Corinthian community (Horsley 2011). However, the precise nature of these divisions has been a subject of extensive scholarly debate. In the nineteenth century, Baur advanced a particularly influential and controversial interpretation, focusing on the so-called "Christ party" (*die Christuspartei*). Baur argued that the divisions in Corinth did not consist of four distinct groups, but rather two major factions: one representing Jewish Christians (associated with Peter and Christ) and the other representing Gentile Christians (associated with Paul and Apollos). According to Baur, the "Judaizers" in Corinth were Paul's primary adversaries, and the divisions were rooted in a conflict between Jewish and Gentile Christians (Baur 2021). However, Baur's theory has been criticized for its antisemitic overtones, and while some scholars have continued to develop variations of his argument (Barrett 1971; Vielhauer 1975; Goulder 1991), most have moved beyond the proposed Jewish-Christian vs. Gentile-Christian framework. Numerous other theories have been advanced to explain the diversity in Corinth (Kwon 2010: 2), with John Kloppenborg's assertion that "factionalism is clearly a problem at Corinth" (Kloppenborg 2011: 192) representing a common view among contemporary scholars.

I, however, would suggest—following Nils A. Dahl's proposal—that the root of the problem in 1 Corinthians 1–4 is not necessarily factionalism per se, but rather the Corinthians' rejection of Paul's authority. Dahl argues that these chapters are primarily "an apology for Paul," meaning that Paul's main concern is to defend his apostolic authority against opposition within the Corinthian church (Dahl 1967). Paul is not battling Judaizers or engaging in doctrinal disputes, as Baur suggested; rather, says Dahl, he is trying to reassert his authority over a community that seems to be questioning it. This becomes evident in 1 Corinthians 4:18, where Paul mentions that "some people" in Corinth—whom he labels "arrogant"—believe he is not returning to Corinth. These individuals appear to be challenging Paul's leadership, prompting him to defend his apostleship (1 Cor. 4:19). Paul's concern with their rejection of his authority 1 Corinthians 9:3 emphasizes further. There, Paul writes: "This is my defense (ἀπολογία) to those who would examine me." Clearly, Paul's authority is being challenged here.

Dahl's argument gains support from the rhetorical strategies Paul employs in these chapters. For example, Paul frequently emphasizes that he did not come to Corinth with "eloquent wisdom" (1 Cor. 1:17) or "lofty words" (1 Cor. 2:1), nor did he use "persuasive wisdom" (1 Cor. 2:4). These statements likely reflect criticisms leveled against Paul by some Corinthians, who may have valued rhetorical skill and philosophical sophistication. Rather than refute this criticism directly, Paul embraces it, arguing that his lack of rhetorical polish only serves to highlight the power of the gospel, which does not depend on human wisdom (1 Cor. 2:5). In doing so, Paul redefines the terms of the debate: it is not about who is the most eloquent or persuasive, but about who faithfully preaches the message of Christ.

Yet Dahl's description of the Corinthians as people who "thought themselves inspired, pneumatic persons" (Dahl 1967: 321) might not fully capture the situation. Paul's comment that he could not address the Corinthians as "spiritual people (πνευματικοί)" (1 Cor. 3:1) seems to reflect his own assessment of their spiritual maturity, rather than their self-understanding. In this sense, Paul's portrayal of the Corinthians may reveal more about his concerns than about their actual beliefs or behavior.

One of the intriguing aspects of the Corinthian controversy is that the divisions Paul describes in 1 Corinthians are entirely absent from the account in Acts. The book of Acts, which narrates Paul's time in Corinth, does not mention any internal strife within the church. This raises an important question: if the divisions were as severe as Paul suggests, why does Acts remain silent about them? Some might argue that the events in Acts took place before the divisions emerged, but this explanation is not entirely satisfactory. Acts does record the arrival of Apollos in Corinth (Acts 19:1), which many scholars believe occurred around the same time Paul wrote 1 Corinthians, yet it makes no mention of the Corinthian church being divided over Paul and Apollos, as 1 Corinthians 3:4 indicates. Instead, Acts emphasizes *external* opposition to Paul, particularly from the Jewish community (Acts 18:6, 12-17). This raises the possibility that the opposition Paul faced in Corinth continued even after he left and was not limited to internal church disputes. Perhaps what Paul describes as internal division was, in fact, an ongoing resistance to his authority that persisted after his departure.

Paul's Concern: Authority, Not Division

When one closely examines the slogans mentioned in 1 Corinthians 1:11-12, it becomes clear that Paul is not particularly interested in elaborating on the details of the different factions. After briefly stating what he has heard about the divisions, he quickly shifts the focus to himself, writing: "Has Christ been divided? Was Paul crucified for you? Or were you baptized in the name of Paul? I thank God that I baptized none of you except Crispus and Gaius, so that no one can say that you were baptized in my name" (1 Cor. 1:13-14). Notice that only the first question concerns Christ, while the rest are focused on himself. This suggests that Paul's main concern is not division per se, but his unease with the rejection of his authority. As Dahl points out, the slogan "I belong to Christ" is not necessarily the motto of a distinct Christ party but could simply mean "I belong to Christ—and therefore I am independent of Paul" (Dahl 1967). This same logic could apply to the slogans "I belong to Apollos" and "I belong to Cephas," reflecting the Corinthians' reluctance to give Paul sole authority over their community.

It seems the Corinthians valued a diversity of leadership and theological perspectives, preferring a range of teachers and leaders, some of whom they found as compelling—if not more so—than Paul. For them, Paul was not the only option. As Laura Nasrallah puts it, 1 Corinthians "reveals that those addressed did not always agree with Paul's arguments and turned to others for advice and leadership" (Nasrallah 2021: 350). However, Paul sought full allegiance to his authority, making this not just a theological disagreement but a political struggle for control. As Welborn suggests, the Corinthians' resistance to Paul can be seen as a struggle for difference against the unifying authority that Paul represented (Welborn 1987).

Paul's assertion that he did not baptize many in Corinth is a crucial point in his argument to deflect attention from the significance of baptism as a source of authority. In 1 Corinthians 1:14, Paul states, "I thank God that I baptized none of you except Crispus and Gaius," followed by a series of rhetorical questions in verse 13: "Has Christ been divided? Was Paul crucified for you? Were you baptized in the name of Paul?" These questions are structured to elicit a negative response, pointing away from Paul himself and redirecting the community's focus to Christ. Paul's emphasis on this distinction minimizes his role in the ritual of baptism, positioning Christ—and not the leaders—as the central figure of their faith.

However, as Richard Hays notes, there may have been deeper misunderstandings within the Corinthian community about the significance of baptism. Hays suggests that the Corinthians might have viewed baptism not just as a spiritual initiation, but as establishing a personal and hierarchical bond between the baptized individual and the baptizer, much like a patron–client relationship in the Greco-Roman world (Hays 2011). In such a view, the act of baptism would confer loyalty and authority upon the baptizer, creating factions or allegiances based on who performed the rite. This likely contributed to the divisions in the church, as members aligned themselves with the particular leaders who had baptized them, reinforcing the sense of rivalry and competition between different groups within the community.

Faced with this situation, Paul seeks to disconnect leadership and power from the ritual of baptism. Rather than grounding his authority in the act of baptism, which was perhaps the strategy of other leaders in Corinth, Paul shifts the focus entirely. He thanks God that he baptized only a few people, deliberately distancing himself from any claims that his authority comes from performing the ritual. In doing so, Paul undermines the notion that baptism binds people to a specific leader and redirects the Corinthians to the essence of his ministry: the proclamation of the gospel.

Paul frames his authority around what he calls "gospelizing" (εὐαγγελίζεσθαι), the act of preaching the good news (1 Cor. 1:17). This strategic shift from ritual to proclamation reveals how central speech and discourse are in Paul's understanding of authority. For Paul, leadership in the community is not based on ritual acts like baptism, which could foster factionalism, but on the effective communication and preaching of the gospel message. As Elizabeth Castelli argues, Paul's authority is rooted not in his possession of an uncontestable truth but in his ability to establish himself as an authoritative speaker in a context where his leadership is contested (Castelli 1991). His rhetorical maneuver is to shift the focus from ritual practice to speech, where he can more effectively assert his leadership in a way that transcends the diverse allegiances created by baptism.

In this sense, Paul's authority is built not on the ritual acts that others may use to consolidate power, but on his ability to present the gospel and position himself as a messenger of divine truth. His approach enables him to contest and redefine the power structures in the Corinthian community, emphasizing that it is the message of the cross, rather than who performs the baptism, that should unite the believers. By distancing himself from the act of baptism, Paul is able to reclaim a different form of authority—one that is rooted in the message itself rather than in the leader who performs a particular rite.

Paul and Apollos

In 1 Corinthians 3, Paul revisits the issues of jealousy and quarrelling among the Corinthians, but this time he narrows the focus to himself and Apollos. While he had initially mentioned four groups in 1 Corinthians 1:12 (Paul, Apollos, Cephas, and Christ), he now speaks only of two: "For when one says, 'I belong to Paul,' and another, 'I belong to Apollos,' are you not merely human?" (1 Cor. 3:4). Why this shift from four factions to two? Some scholars have suggested that the real conflict in Corinth was between Paul and Apollos, with Apollos emerging as the main troublemaker (Campbell 2002). For his part, C. K. Barrett has argued that the Apollos party may have exaggerated certain elements of Apollos's teaching, particularly his emphasis on wisdom (σοφία), which Paul critiques in chapters 2 and 3 (Barrett 2003). Paul uses two analogies—planting and building—to describe his relationship with Apollos. He emphasizes that both he and Apollos are merely "servants" (διάκονοι) through whom the Corinthians came to believe, each playing a complementary role as directed by the Lord (1 Cor. 3:5). "I planted, Apollos watered, but God gave the growth," Paul writes (1 Cor. 3:6), positioning himself and Apollos as co-workers (συνεργοί), while reminding the Corinthians that it is God who ultimately produces the results.

Paul immediately shifts from the planting analogy to that of building (1 Cor. 3:10-15). In this analogy, Paul portrays himself as a "wise architect" (σοφὸς ἀρχιτέκτων), laying the foundation (Christ) on which others build. However, Apollos is conspicuously absent from this section; Paul is now the sole focus. As Gaventa observes, while Paul initially claims that he and Apollos are mere servants, his subsequent imagery casts him in a much more authoritative role as the architect who laid the foundation (Gaventa 2017). This irony is further compounded by Paul's use of the word σοφὸς (wise) to describe himself, despite his earlier rejection of worldly wisdom (1 Cor. 3:18) only further compounds this irony. The tension between Paul's critique of wisdom and his self-portrayal as a wise builder underscores the rhetorical complexity of his argument.

Paul's discussion of Apollos resumes in 1 Corinthians 3:21-23, where he urges the Corinthians not to boast about human leaders: "So let no one boast about human leaders. For all things are yours, whether Paul or Apollos or Cephas or the world or life or death or the present or the future—all belong to you, and you belong to Christ, and Christ belongs to God" (1 Cor. 3:21-23). This is a striking statement, as Paul seems to downplay the importance of human leadership, including his own. However, as Witherington notes, this is a rhetorical reversal: after emphasizing his foundational role, Paul now includes himself, Apollos, and Cephas as belonging to the Corinthians, signaling that they should not place any leader above the others (Witherington III 1995). Yet, this rhetorical reversal should be understood in light of Paul's larger goal: to reassert his authority in a community where it is being questioned. By placing himself on the same level as Apollos and Cephas, Paul is making a strategic move to ensure that the Corinthians recognize his equal (if not superior) status.

The seemingly disconnected list of items in verse 22 (the world, life, death, the present, and the future) may appear unnecessary, but it serves to emphasize Paul's Stoic-like point that all things belong to the Corinthians. Yet, Paul concludes by reminding them that they ultimately belong to Christ, and Christ belongs to God, thus grounding their identity and unity in the larger divine hierarchy.

In Closing

Paul's description of the situation in 1 Corinthians 1–4 is based on a secondary report, a factor that we must take seriously in our analysis of the conflict. What we have in 1 Corinthians is not a direct, unmediated portrayal of who the Corinthians are or what is happening within the community, but rather Paul's own interpretation of events as relayed to him by Chloe's people. This introduces two layers of representation: the initial report from Chloe's people, and Paul's subsequent response to that report. These layers highlight the complexity of the situation, as we are seeing Corinth through Paul's lens.

Paul's words make clear that his authority over the community has diminished. The Corinthians are challenging his leadership and aligning themselves with other figures of influence, indicating a shift away from Paul as their primary leader. As Fee aptly points out:

> [T]he *historical situation* in Corinth was *one of conflict between the church and its founder*. This is not to deny that the church was experiencing internal strife, but it is to argue that the greater problem of 'division' was between Paul and some in the community who were leading the church as a whole into an anti-Pauline view of things.
>
> (Italic is his. Fee 1988: 6)

This suggests that the divisions in the Corinthian church are not only about theological differences or social dynamics within the community, but also about a broader struggle over leadership and authority. Paul's letter reveals his internal struggle to maintain his influence over a church that has begun to look elsewhere for guidance. In essence, Paul was no longer the central figure in their communal life; he had become merely one leader among many.

The issue at stake in 1 Corinthians, then, is not solely about doctrinal matters or the content of the gospel. Rather, it is about how Paul strategically uses the gospel to assert and reestablish his authority within a community that was growing increasingly distant from his leadership. His focus on unity and allegiance to Christ, while certainly genuine, also reflects his desire to realign the community under his apostolic influence, addressing the power dynamics that had shifted in Corinth.

4

Consolidating Authority Amidst Oppositions

In the previous chapter, we explored the dynamics of factionalism within the Corinthian community. But we discovered that the root of the issue extends beyond internal divisions. At its core, the conflict centers on a struggle between Paul and certain members of the community who challenge his authority and question his message. Far from being a neutral mediator, Paul is an active participant in this conflict, as it directly involves his leadership. He urges the Corinthians to unite, calling for the absence of divisions and appealing for them to be "of the same mind and the same purpose" (1:10). This plea for unity is not a mere abstract ideal but a strategic response to the resistance Paul faces from those who contest his authority. As Margaret Mitchell aptly notes, this emphasis on unity functions as the "thesis" of the entire letter (Mitchell 1991: 68–80). However, Paul's pursuit of unity is hardly impartial; it is driven by his desire to solidify his leadership in the face of opposition.

Gospelizing

In clarifying his role in Corinth, Paul insists that he was sent not to baptize but to preach the gospel (1:17). His claim appears to be a response to the fact that some in Corinth are aligning themselves with particular leaders—whether Apollos or Cephas—based on who baptized them (1:12–13). This division among the Corinthians is not an abstract issue; it reflects the community's struggle over authority and identity, which Paul seeks to address. By stating that he was sent not to baptize but to preach, Paul attempts to shift the focus away from the individuals and practices that might further divide the community and toward the message he wishes to convey.

But what is this message? For Paul, the gospel is centered on "the cross of Christ" (1:17) or "the message about the cross" (1:18). This is where the tension between Paul and the Corinthians becomes particularly evident. To the Corinthians, who lived under Roman rule, the cross—an instrument of Roman power and punishment—was an improbable and unsettling foundation for the gospel. They were well acquainted with the harsh realities of crucifixion, a practice that symbolized not only humiliation and suffering but also submission to imperial authority. The visible ruins of Hellenistic Corinth served as constant reminders of Rome's brutal domination. As Sean Adams explains, crucifixion was a public spectacle that Rome used to maintain order and enforce compliance (Adams 2008: 112). For the Corinthians, the cross was therefore primarily not a beacon of hope but a tool of terror, designed to intimidate and suppress those who challenged Roman power.

Paul's insistence that the cross is central to the gospel likely conflicted with the Corinthians' expectations of power and success. How could the cross—an instrument of torture—be considered good news? For the Corinthians, this message would have seemed both counterintuitive and offensive. Crucifixion was the lowest form of punishment, reserved for criminals and rebels. To identify with such a symbol would have been understood as aligning oneself with weakness and failure, not with the strength and victory they may have expected. This tension is particularly evident when Paul acknowledges that his message of the cross would be a "stumbling block" for Jews and "foolishness" for Gentiles (1:23). The Corinthians, steeped in Roman and Greek values, would have struggled to accept a message that seemed to celebrate defeat rather than power.

Martin Hengel describes the inherent contradiction in Paul's message, noting that "a crucified messiah, son of God or God, must have seemed a contradiction in terms to anyone—Jew, Greek, Roman, or barbarian—asked to believe such a claim, and it will certainly have been thought offensive and foolish" (Hengel 1977: 10). This offense and confusion likely fueled the resistance Paul faced in Corinth. Some Corinthians may have viewed Paul's focus on the cross as an indication of his weakness or inability to align with the more powerful and successful ideologies of their time. Richard Hays adds that "to proclaim a crucified Messiah is to talk nonsense" (Hays 2011: 30), further underscoring the difficulty Paul encountered when trying to convey his message to the Corinthians.

Rather than a harmonious relationship, Paul's engagement with the Corinthians reflects a struggle over how they should understand power, leadership, and the gospel itself. The conflict is not only about doctrine but also about identity and the values the community should embrace. While Paul emphasizes the cross as the central message, some Corinthians may have resisted this because it clashed with their own expectations of strength and victory in a society shaped by Roman ideals.

The tension between Paul and the Corinthians is evident in how Paul's message about the cross directly challenges the cultural and social values of the Roman world. For the Corinthians, who were navigating life under Roman rule, Paul's insistence on embracing the cross may have seemed out of touch with their lived realities. Paul's struggle, then, is not just with the theological implications of the cross but with the cultural conflict it provokes among his audience. He is aware that his message will not be easily accepted, and his call for unity is an attempt to align the community with a vision that some evidently found difficult to embrace.

In this light, the conflict between Paul and the Corinthians is not merely about doctrinal disagreements but also about competing visions of what it means to be a community in the Roman world. Paul's emphasis on the cross represents a challenge to the values of power and honor that many in Corinth may have held. His uphill battle is not only about asserting his own authority but about convincing the Corinthians to adopt a perspective that runs counter to the dominant culture in which they live.

Socio-Economic Argument

To build his case, Paul takes an interesting argumentative approach by focusing on the socio-economic condition of the Corinthians. He writes, "Consider your own call, brothers and sisters; not many of you were wise by human standards (Greek: κατὰ σάρκα), not many were powerful, not many were of noble birth" (1:26). Ben Witherington argues that the term "calling" in this context refers to their socio-economic status rather than a religious calling (Witherington III 1995: 113). Given that Paul recognizes the negative perception of the cross, persuading the Corinthians to accept both him and his message of the cross poses a significant challenge. Paul likely anticipates some Corinthians dismissing him and saying, "No, it's not worth following you and your foolish message."

Defending his message of the cross, Paul urges them to "see" (βλέπετε) or, as Thiselton suggests, more forcefully to "think about" (Thiselton 2013: 179) their calling. In other words, if they are inclined to reject Paul's message, he calls on them to reflect on their own socio-economic condition, reminding them that their condition is not so different from the cross itself. By doing so, Paul underscores the idea that the Corinthians, like the cross, embody what is considered lowly and despised in the eyes of the world.

This strategy, often considered *ad hominem*, targets the Corinthians' identity by aligning their condition with the apparent foolishness of the cross. Paul builds his argument by drawing a parallel between their socio-economic status and the nature of the cross. He does not simply present the cross as a theological abstraction but instead connects it directly to the Corinthians' lived reality. The comparison between the cross and the Corinthians becomes evident in these verses:

1:25—The Cross	1:27—The Corinthians
For God's foolishness is wiser than human wisdom, and God's weakness is stronger than human strength (NRSV).	But God chose what is foolish in the world to shame the wise; God chose what is weak in the world to shame the strong (NRSV).

On the one hand, the cross represents God's foolishness, while on the other, the Corinthians represent the foolishness of the world. The logic is straightforward: if God can choose the Corinthians, viewed as foolish by worldly standards, to shame the wise, then God can choose the cross to reveal divine wisdom. Similarly, if God can choose the weak Corinthians to shame the strong, then the same logic applies to the cross. The Corinthians, therefore, become living examples of what God can accomplish through apparent weakness and foolishness. Verse 28 reinforces this point: "God chose what is low and despised in the world, things that are not, to reduce to nothing things that are, so that no one might boast in the presence of God." Paul essentially tells them that if they can accept their own lowly status, they should not be surprised by his focus on the cross.

But how are the actual socio-economic conditions of the Corinthian followers of Jesus? Let us look closer. This area of study has become a focal point of scholarly debate over the past two decades. In 2004, Steven J. Friesen published an influential essay on poverty in Pauline studies, challenging the prevailing consensus that the social composition of Pauline churches represented a "cross-section of society" (esp. Meeks 2003; Theissen 2004). By "cross-section," scholars refer to a social group comprising individuals from middle and lower sections, characterized by upward mobility (Meeks 2003: 73). Meeks builds his case mainly on the category of "status" as an analytical tool to measure their social stratification (Meeks 2003: 53–5).

Yet Friesen critiques the use of "status," arguing that it is an unhelpful category. Not only is it too broad—encompassing ethnicity, gender, wealth, citizenship, and more—it is also nearly impossible to quantify, he says. Moreover, he argues that this focus on status has caused scholars to overlook the issue of poverty. As Friesen states, "The way social analysis is practiced in the so-called new consensus ... actually draws our attention away from poverty" (Friesen 2004: 334). Consequently, discussions of class conflict and economic oppression are largely absent from Pauline scholarship. Friesen describes this approach as "capitalist criticism" (Friesen 2004: 336), suggesting that scholars have inadvertently created an image of early Christians shaped by capitalist assumptions.

Friesen proposes an alternative method for understanding the socio-economic conditions of individuals in Pauline churches through what he calls "the poverty scale" (Friesen 2004: 340). Various scholars have adopted, adapted, and modified this framework (Horrell 2009; Longenecker 2009, 2010; Rosenfeld and Perlmutter 2011). However, the core structure of his argument and categorization continues to serve as a useful tool for examining the economic conditions of early Christians (cf. Barclay 2004: 364–5). Friesen's breakdown of this poverty scale is as follows:

Scale	Category	% of population
PS1	Imperial elites	0.04%
PS2	Regional elites	1.00%
PS3	Municipal elites	1.76%
PS4	Moderate surplus	7%?
PS5	Stable near subsistence	22%?
PS6	At subsistence	40%
PS7	Below subsistence	28%

In short, the majority of the population in the Greco-Roman world lived at the lower end of the socio-economic spectrum. Approximately 90 percent of the population falls within the PS5 to PS7 categories of Friesen's poverty scale. Paul and the Corinthians would likely be situated within these levels. Friesen's detailed analysis of names associated with individuals in Corinth further underscores the prevalence of poverty in Pauline churches. Below is an adapted table from Friesen's more extensive data (Friesen 2004: 357):

Name	Reference	PS
Chloe	1 Cor. 1:11	4
Gaius	Rom. 16:23	4
Erastus	Rom. 16:23	4–5
The household of Stephanas	1 Cor. 16:15–16	5–6
(Many) saints in Corinth	1 Cor. 16:1–2	5–6
(Many) saints in Corinth	2 Cor. 8:12–15	6
Paul	2 Cor. 11:1–21	6
Those who do not have food for the Lord's Supper	1 Cor. 11: 22	6–7

This list, of course, does not represent the entirety of Christ followers in Corinth—and Friesen is fully aware of this limitation (Friesen 2004: 332). However, it does offer insight into the socio-economic condition of the Corinthian community. They are predominantly a poor group of people, belonging to "the underbelly of Roman society," to use Boykin Sanders' phrase (Sanders 2007: 282). Even Paul himself was likely a man of modest means (cf. Meggitt 2000: 77), as Friesen notes, "an itinerant worker who supported himself by physical labor" (Friesen 2004: 359).

Returning to Paul's insistence that the cross mirrors the Corinthian socio-economic condition, a few observations can be made. First, as a poor person himself, Paul could have pointed to his own life and calling and have said, "Think about me and my call ...." But he does not. Instead, he directs the Corinthians to consider their own situation. In doing so, he not only reminds them of their identity but also subtly puts them in their place. However, this rhetoric also reveals a deeper sense of insecurity in Paul. He is keenly aware that his message is not popular, and that he, as the messenger, is not particularly compelling. Just a few lines after urging them to reflect on themselves, Paul admits: "I came to you in weakness and in fear and in much trembling. My speech and my proclamation were not with plausible words of wisdom, but with a demonstration of the Spirit and of power, so that your faith might rest not on human wisdom but on the power of God" (2:3–5). Both the message and the messenger present problems for the Corinthians. When reading 1 Corinthians, it is important for us as readers to remember that Paul, too, is grappling with his own limitations and shortcomings. This is a letter that cuts both ways, reflecting the struggles of both the Corinthians and Paul himself.

Second, the socio-economic discussion further complicates Paul's claim that "God chose what is foolish in the world to shame the wise and what is weak in the world to shame the strong" (1:27). While this may sound like a countercultural statement, from the Corinthians' perspective it might appear disconnected from their daily struggles. Who exactly are the foolish who have shamed the wise, and who are the weak who have shamed the strong? Paul does not provide clear answers. Is he referring to upward mobility? Such social movement was rare in the Greco-Roman world (Friesen 2010). Or is he talking about a social revolution? Paul does not seem to be advocating for such a shift, as his overall tone suggests a desire to maintain the existing social structures, albeit tempered by Christian love. Gerd Theissen addresses this tension by describing Paul's stance as "love-patriarchalism," which "takes social differences for granted but ameliorates them through an obligation of respect and love" (Theissen 2004: 107). Similarly, Dale Martin describes this as "benevolent patriarchalism" (Martin 1999: 42). Rather than pushing for societal change, Paul seems to be working within the existing structures.

Third, Paul continues his argument by stating, "God chose what is low and despised in the world, things that are not, to reduce to nothing things that are, so that no one might boast in the presence of God" (1:27). This rhetoric is crucial for him, as he likely believed that some Corinthians felt they were too elevated or sophisticated for the message of the cross. The fact that some of them rejected him and his message likely stemmed from their perception that aligning with the cross—a symbol of weakness and shame—

would undermine their status and social standing. For those who considered themselves wise or powerful by worldly standards, Paul's emphasis on the cross may have seemed not only inappropriate but also demeaning to their sense of identity.

The Indonesian language uses the word *belagu* to describe someone who is prideful or boastful, particularly when they refuse something because they feel it is beneath them. When an Indonesian says, "*Jangan belagu!*" it means "Don't think too highly of yourself" or "Don't act like you're too good for something." Paul seems to fear that some Corinthians might act *belagu*, rejecting his message of the cross because they regard themselves as being above such a humiliating symbol. He wants to put them in their place. The Corinthians, in turn, might have responded, "We don't need to be *belagu* to think the cross is shameful, ugly, and cruel. Almost everyone in Corinth agrees that your fixation on the cross is indeed scandalous and foolish." This ongoing power struggle between Paul and the Corinthians forms the foundation for understanding the dynamics at play in 1 Corinthians. Paul's use of such strong rhetoric reveals the depth of the challenge he faced in persuading the Corinthians to embrace a gospel that ran counter to their cultural and social expectations.

Parental Authority

Paul is acutely aware that the Corinthians are challenging his authority. In this letter, he seeks to reestablish his position as their leader—the one they must follow. He not only perceives them as prideful but also suspects that they consider themselves "mature" (2:6). One of Paul's strategies to counter this is by evoking the language of parenthood, thereby reinforcing a hierarchical relationship. He positions himself as the parent and the Corinthians as the children. Interestingly, Paul not only assumes the role of a father but also employs maternal imagery (3:2). As Grace Emmett describes, this reflects a form of "maternal masculinity" (Emmett 2021). Two key passages worth examining are 3:1–3a, where Paul adopts a maternal image, and 4:14–15, where he portrays himself as a father.

A Breastfeeding Mother

In 3:1–3a, Paul describes the Corinthians as "infants in Christ," contrasting them with the "mature" who are capable of understanding his message (2:6). He argues that the wisdom he preaches comes from God and is revealed through the Spirit (2:1–11). Only those who receive this wisdom through the Spirit can truly comprehend it, while those who remain on a merely physical level (ψυχικός; 4:14) perceive God's gifts as foolishness (μωρία). Here, Paul contrasts the ψυχικός (natural or physical) with the πνευματικὸς (spiritual) in 4:14–15. A spiritual person will understand and accept his message (2:13), whereas those still operating on a physical level will reject it. Paul's portrayal of the Corinthians as "infants" extends this discussion of the natural versus the spiritual. They are considered infants (νηπίοι) because their spiritual immaturity prevents them from fully grasping his teachings.

After describing the Corinthians as infants, it is no surprise that Paul immediately likens himself to a breastfeeding mother, stating, "I fed you with milk, not solid food, for you were not ready for solid food" (3:2). This metaphor reinforces Paul's position as their nurturing caregiver. In her study of this maternal image, Beverly Gaventa argues that some Corinthians might have challenged Paul's masculinity, suggesting he was not a "real man," and that the use of this image may have been shocking to their gender expectations. I find Gaventa's argument regarding Paul's use of maternal imagery compelling, particularly her emphasis on how this image challenges traditional gender assumptions and highlights the complexity of Paul's self-understanding within the broader Greco-Roman social framework (Gaventa 1996: 47).

But what is the rhetorical goal of employing this maternal imagery? Gaventa contends that rather than reading it in light of the previous discussion on maturity and infancy in chapter 2, we should view it through the lens of Paul's "apostolic role" in chapters 3 and 4. According to Gaventa, Paul addresses the Corinthians' divisiveness by using analogies of planting and building (3:5–16) to demonstrate that "the Corinthians belong, not to Paul or Apollos, but to Christ, as becomes clear in v. 23: "You belong to Christ"" (Gaventa 1996: 49). Through these analogies, Paul seeks to show that he "is not the authoritative ruler" (Gaventa 1996: 49). Paul's use of the image of a nursing mother must be understood in this context. For, as Gaventa argues, "The metaphor expresses the bond of affection and care that characterizes the relationship and simultaneously places Paul at the margins of what is perceived to be 'genuine' manhood" (Gaventa 1996: 50)

While I am sympathetic to Gaventa's insistence that this metaphor is countercultural, I diverge from her interpretation in two key ways. First, I question her portrayal of the Corinthians as divisive. While Paul certainly addresses conflicts and factionalism in 1 Corinthians, I do not believe these divisions define the Corinthian community. Instead, I suggest that these tensions reflect the broader social dynamics at play in a diverse and complex urban environment like Corinth, where cultural, social, and economic differences likely contributed to moments of discord. Second, although I acknowledge the value of reading this metaphor in light of Paul's apostolic role in chapters 3 and 4, I do not think we should entirely abandon reading it from the perspective of the discussion of maturity and infancy from chapter 2. Paul is indeed concerned with maturity and spiritual growth, as we have already noted. Therefore, the image of the mother here not only conveys a humble and servant-like Paul but also an authoritative and controlling figure. It is a double-edged image.

Through the use of maternal imagery, Paul elevates himself to being the primary source of spiritual nourishment and wisdom, emphasizing his unique role in shaping the spiritual growth of the Corinthians. This metaphor of breastfeeding is particularly striking, as it frames Paul not merely as a passive caregiver but as one not only actively involved in their development, but also as indispensable to their growth as infants to maturity. As Emmett observes, Paul is "authoritative and instructional" in his interactions with the Corinthians, a stance that contrasts with the gentler approach he adopts with the Thessalonians (Emmett 2021: 21). The image of breastfeeding amplifies this, as in the Greco-Roman world breastfeeding was often associated with pedagogy and character formation (Myers 2017; Emmett 2021: 22). By likening himself to a mother who provides milk, Paul is not only portraying himself as nurturing but also as instructing, using this maternal role to assert his control over their lives. The Corinthians, like infants, are dependent on him for their sustenance, unable to grow without his guidance.

However, this maternal metaphor also raises important questions about Paul's legitimacy. By assuming this authoritative role, Paul implicitly invites scrutiny regarding the source of his authority. The Corinthians might naturally question, "Who gave you this role as our mother? Who authorized you to dictate our spiritual nourishment?" While Paul claims that his authority comes from Christ (see 1:1, 10, 17), the Corinthians may not have been universally accepted this claim. Some of them likely viewed him as a self-appointed leader struggling to maintain his influence over a community among whom he no longer lived. His absence from Corinth, combined with his reliance on such a bold metaphor to assert control, may have amplified their doubts about his right to lead and direct their spiritual lives. The very metaphor Paul uses to claim authority could be seen as a point of contention, with some Corinthians potentially questioning whether his position as their "mother" was legitimate or whether he was attempting to reassert authority over a community that had begun to outgrow his influence.

A Father

While Paul adopts the role of a mother in chapter 3, he shifts to the role of a father in 4:14–16. He writes, "I am not writing this to make you ashamed, but to admonish you as my beloved children. For though you might have ten thousand guardians in Christ, you do not have many fathers. Indeed, in Christ Jesus I became your father through the gospel." This paternal claim is another attempt to assert his authority, positioning himself as the primary figure in their lives. As Eva Maria Lassen states: "For Paul, the use of the father-image seems to have been a fundamental one for expressing his relationship to the congregations, which he had founded" (Lassen 1991: 127). However, even as Paul tries to soften his tone, this paternal language might come off as condescending. His claim to fatherhood reinforces the hierarchical relationship he wishes to establish.

It's difficult to say with certainty whether Paul's apparent attempt to soften his language by calling the Corinthians "beloved children" (4:14) would actually have comforted them, especially considering the tension between him and the community. The use of the adjective "beloved" is clearly an attempt to cushion what might otherwise feel like a condescending or paternalistic statement. However, calling them his "children" may not have been received well, especially by a community already questioning his authority. For a group that prides itself on wisdom, independence, and perhaps even spiritual maturity, Paul's parental language could have felt patronizing, reinforcing a power imbalance with which they were already uncomfortable.

From the Corinthians' perspective, being called "children" might have heightened their sense of being belittled. This is particularly true if they were among those who thought themselves spiritually advanced or more aligned with other leaders, like Apollos or Cephas, whom they perhaps perceived as more respectable or authoritative than Paul. Even though Paul uses the term "beloved," the paternal dynamic he sets up emphasizes their dependence on him for spiritual guidance and maturity, which they might have resented. This hierarchical language could have widened the divide between Paul and the Corinthians, making them feel less like equals in Christ and more like subordinates under Paul's authority.

As a reader, imagining the Corinthians' reaction requires us to consider the broader context of their strained relationship. Paul's tone throughout much of 1 Corinthians fluctuates between harsh criticism and appeals for unity, reflecting his frustration with the community. Given their likely skepticism of his leadership, it's possible that the Corinthians would not have been comforted by his attempt to call them "beloved children" (4:14) but might instead have felt alienated by what they could have perceived as a power move—Paul asserting his superiority as both their spiritual father and mother.

Ultimately, while Paul's intention might have been to mend the rift, the Corinthians' reception of his language would have depended on whether they accepted his authority. For those already inclined to resist him, this parental metaphor could have solidified their resistance, reinforcing their perception that Paul was trying to control them rather than engage them as equals. This leads to the next way Paul asserts his dominance: demanding that they imitate him.

Imitation

Throughout 1 Corinthians, Paul issues a direct command to the Corinthians to imitate him, twice urging them to follow his example. Two key texts, 1 Cor. 4:16 and 11:1, encapsulate the thrust of this exhortation:

> I appeal to you, then, be imitators of me.
>
> (4:16)

> Be imitators of me, as I am of Christ.
>
> (11:1)

In Paul's broader rhetorical strategy, his call to imitation is a calculated move to reinforce his political control over the Corinthian community. The repeated use of "imitate me" in 1 Corinthians underscores a power dynamic, revealing Paul's intent to assert his leadership and influence over the assembly. In chapter 4, Paul sets the stage by acknowledging that while they may have countless guardians (παιδαγωγούς), they do not have many fathers—only one. At this juncture, the Corinthians might assume that "father" refers to God, given the religious tradition of divine fatherhood. However, Paul overturns this expectation by boldly claiming that it is he, not God, who holds this unique position. This maneuver effectively elevates Paul's authority, asserting that his relationship to the Corinthians is singular and indispensable, thus positioning himself at the center of their social and communal order.

Paul's insistence on being their only father is not simply about spiritual kinship; it is a strategic move to consolidate his control. By claiming this paternal role, Paul is demanding their allegiance and obedience, effectively neutralizing any challenges to his authority. His command to "imitate me" further reinforces this control by urging the Corinthians to conform to his example, aligning their behavior and loyalties with his leadership. It is ultimately about political dominance. By making himself the model for imitation, Paul seeks to establish a system of influence where his authority is unquestioned. The appeal to fatherhood and imitation is thus a tool for maintaining power over the community, ensuring that the Corinthians remain loyal to his leadership and vision, rather than seeking alternative sources of authority within their diverse and contentious assembly.

Elizabeth Castelli argues that Paul's call to "imitate me" should be understood within the existing power structure of Corinth. For Paul, difference is perceived as a threat to his authority and to the community's cohesion. While many have attempted to spiritualize this command, Castelli emphasizes that urging others to imitate someone is inherently a political act, one aimed at rejecting differences that could undermine Paul's leadership. Castelli writes, "The ideological force of such a prescription [to be the same] is clear; if imitation and the drive toward sameness are exhorted and celebrated, then difference is perceived as problematic, dangerous, threatening" (Castelli 1991: 22). Thus, Paul's directive is not merely about moral or spiritual guidance; it is a means of enforcing uniformity to consolidate his control.

Drawing on Epictetus' description of the father as a military general, Castelli further argues that Paul's paternal mimetic assertion in the Greco-Roman world echoes the role of a father "possessing total authority over children" (Castelli 1991: 101). Paul's demand for imitation, then, reinforces his position as a figure with unquestioned authority, reflecting a social hierarchy in which obedience and conformity are critical to maintaining his power within the Corinthian assembly. The demand for imitation is, in other words, a way to ensure that the Corinthians conform to his likeness, thereby minimizing dissent or alternative perspectives that could undermine his influence. In other words, Paul's appeal for sameness is politically motivated. By urging the Corinthians to imitate him, he is effectively neutralizing the potential for diversity of thought or behavior within the community, which clearly could challenge his authority. This move toward uniformity seems to be an effort to preserve his position of power, as any divergence from his example is perceived as a threat to the stability of the community under his leadership.

This dynamic becomes even more apparent in chapter 11. After addressing the issue of food offered to idols in chapter 10, Paul concludes by stating, "Be imitators of me, as I am of Christ" (11:1). This call for imitation is immediately followed by a commendation: "I commend you because you remember me in everything and maintain the traditions just as I handed them to you" (11:2). Here, Paul reinforces the expectation of conformity not only to his personal example but also to the traditions he has established within the community. By connecting imitation of himself with Christ and praising the Corinthians for adhering to the traditions he instituted, Paul is further solidifying his authority. Commenting on this passage, Joseph Marchal points out:

> If this argument is successful, it establishes Paul's authority in the eyes of the audience, but he is also constructing an image of what it means to be imitating Christ, what it means to belong to his version of a Christ-like community. This establishes what will be an ongoing dynamic of conformity and difference, the potential similarity between parties and a hierarchical order that structures their roles differently.
>
> (Marchal 2014: 96)

This sequence of command and praise underscores Paul's emphasis on sameness and conformity as being central to maintaining his control over the community, leaving little room for divergence or dissent.

The Corinthians' response to Paul's demand for imitation and conformity in this context would likely have been mixed, depending on their individual allegiances and social positions within the community. Some members, particularly those who already supported Paul or had close ties to his authority, may have welcomed his call as a reaffirmation of his leadership and guidance. For these individuals, Paul's commendation of their adherence to tradition would have reinforced their loyalty, further aligning them with his authority and the order he sought to establish.

However, for others, particularly those who were critical of Paul's leadership or felt marginalized by his directives, his call for imitation and uniformity could well have been received with resistance or discomfort.

Paul's insistence on maintaining the traditions "just as I handed them to you" (11:2) could have been seen as an attempt to stifle diversity within the community. Corinth, as a cosmopolitan and socially diverse city, likely contained various cultural and ideological perspectives, and Paul's move to assert himself through the rhetoric of sameness might have clashed with the realities of a community that included different social classes, ethnic groups, and religious backgrounds. For those who found Paul's demands restrictive or out of touch with their own experiences, this call to imitation could have been perceived as a form of overreach, exacerbating existing tensions between Paul and certain factions within the church.

Thus, while some might have embraced Paul's directive as a call to unity, others could have interpreted it as a means of tightening control and limiting diversity, which could have fueled further conflict or division within the Corinthian assembly.

In Closing

Paul's use of rhetorical strategies—whether through familial metaphors, socio-economic arguments, or calls for imitation—demonstrates his careful and even calculated approach to consolidating authority in a divided community. By presenting himself as both mother and father to the Corinthians, he asserts his indispensability for their spiritual growth while reinforcing hierarchical power dynamics. This combination of nurturing and authoritative roles reflects Paul's broader concern: to maintain control over a community that challenges his leadership and resists his message, especially in light of cultural expectations of power and success in Roman Corinth. His insistence on the cross as the heart of the gospel, in contrast to the Corinthian desire for honor and strength, reveals the countercultural nature of his appeal.

However, Paul's attempts to unify the community through calls for conformity and imitation also expose deeper tensions between his vision and the realities of Corinthian life. While his rhetoric of "foolishness" and "weakness" might resonate with some, for others it likely exacerbated feelings of discontent, particularly those who regarded his message as out of touch with their social aspirations. In a city marked by social diversity, cultural complexity, and economic disparity, Paul's demand for sameness could have been perceived as an overreach, restricting the very differences that defined the community. His struggle to enforce unity within such a multifaceted group demonstrates the challenges of maintaining leadership in early Christian assemblies that were navigating the pressures of Roman rule and local customs.

Ultimately, Paul's efforts to consolidate his authority in Corinth raise important questions about leadership, power, and community identity that transcend his historical moment. His struggles reflect not only the complexities of managing factionalism but also the broader challenge of establishing a unified vision—in this case a religious one—in a world shaped by competing values and social structures. As early Christian leaders like Paul sought to form cohesive communities, they were forced to grapple with the tension between unity and diversity, control and freedom. In many ways, these tensions remain relevant today, prompting us to wonder: What does it mean to lead a diverse community? And, how should authority be exercised in ways that respect difference while fostering unity?

5

Sexualized Others and the Rhetoric of Exclusion

After descending an escalator at Trump Tower in New York City on June 16, 2015, Donald J. Trump infamously announced his run for the US presidency. In that announcement, Trump appealed to the American fear of the *other*, especially those others who come via the US southern border. A few lines from the speech continue to be quite controversial and invite all kinds of comment:

> When Mexico sends its people, they're not sending their best. They're not sending you. They're not sending you. They're sending people that have lots of problems, and they're bringing those problems with us. They're bringing drugs. They're bringing crime. They're rapists. And some, I assume, are good people.[1]

Notice the change from action-oriented statements (they're *bringing* drugs, they're *bringing* crime) to a being-oriented statement (they *are* rapists). How Trump defines these others is as a sexualized term. It describes not merely what they are allegedly *doing*: it is *who they are*. The Mexican immigrants *are* rapists. That "some … are good people" is an afterthought implying that they are an exception.

From where does Trump get this idea? He made it up. Does he know the "they" to whom he refers in this speech? Of course, not. They are merely an imagined "they"—*others*.

At the time, Trump went on: "It's coming from more than Mexico. It's coming from all over South and Latin America, and it's coming probably—probably—from the Middle East." His focus is thus not only on immigrants

---

[1] The full script of Trump's speech can be accessed here: https://www.washingtonpost.com/news/the-fix/wp/2017/06/16/theyre-rapists-presidents-trump-campaign-launch-speech-two-years-later-annotated/

from Mexico. Mexicans are simply an easy target because they are the closest racialized others whom he perceives as *invading* America. Trump's aim is simple: to demonize immigrants. We (implying US citizens) are good, and they (others, especially certain kinds of others) are bad. The outsiders are those whose sexual desire is uncontrolled, perverted, and unnatural. In short, they are sexual monsters. What is the solution to this problem? Trump argued in his final debate with Hillary Clinton on October 19, 2016, that America needs "strong borders," which he thought America could achieve by building walls. "We're going to get them out. We're going to secure the border. And once the border is secured, at a later date, we'll make determination as to the rest. We have some bad hombres and we're going to get them out," he said. For him, removing these "bad hombres" from America is the solution this problem. They are the cancer in American society.

This line of argumentation is hardly unique to US (and specifically far-right Trumpian) politics. We see it in Corinth as well. This chapter of the book examines Paul's sexualized-ethnic discourse of the other, exemplified particularly in "some guy" (Greek: τινα) whose sexuality Paul describes as perverted and whom Paul, like Trump, probably does not even know personally. Paul then proposes the removal of this person from the community, either by killing him or by not associating with him. Paul regards the mere presence of the other as a threat to the community: a little yeast that leavens the whole batch of dough (5:6b-7). But before focusing on Paul's sexualized and ethnicized words, a little background about the city of Corinth.

A Sexualized City?

To fully understand the force of Paul's rhetoric, a little more background on Corinth is necessary. In the ancient world, Corinth had the reputation of being a sexually defiant city. Strabo wrote in his *Geography* that Corinth was known not only as "'wealthy' because of its commerce, since it is situated on the Isthmus and is master of two harbors, of which one leads straight to Asia and the other to Italy" (Strabo, *Geography*, 8.6.20), but as famous for its citizens' sexual activities. In particular, Strabo writes about the temple of Aphrodite there, which was "so rich that it owned more than a thousand temple slaves, courtesans, whom both men and women had dedicated to the goddess" (Strabo, *Geography*, 8.6.21.) It was on account of these temple slaves (ἱερόδουλοι) that so many ships' crews and others came to Corinth and spent their money.

Some scholars have questioned the validity of Strabo's description of Corinth and the existence of sacred prostitution in Corinth (Conzelmann 1974; Murphy-O'Connor 2002: 56–7). Jerome Murphy-O'Connor, for example, contends that Strabo's description refers to the period prior to

Corinth's destruction by the Romans. He further argues that the temple of Aphrodite would have been too small to accommodate the large number of sacred prostitutes Strabo describes (Murphy-O'Connor 2002: 56). He suggests instead, "What appears to have happened is that Strabo combined elements from a number of different sources to produce a totally distorted picture" (Murphy-O'Connor 2002: 56).

Murphy-O'Connor is right that Corinth had "a certain reputation in sexual matters" (Murphy-O'Connor 2002: 56). Corinth was indeed known widely in the ancient world as a sex city, perhaps a bit like Amsterdam in recent decades. Much as the company Google has spawned the verb "to google," Corinth too spawned a verb—κορινθιάζομαι—which literally means *to Corinth* or *to do the Corinthian thing*. Aristophanes coined this term in the fourth century BCE. In one of the fragments left of his writings, he says: "To 'play the Corinthian' (κορινθιάζομαι) is to consort with prostitutes, from the prostitutes of Corinth, or to be a procurer" (frg. 370). Murphy-O'Connor compiles a helpful list of sources about the reputation of Corinth as a sex city:

> Plays with the title *Korinthiastes*, "The Pimp," were written by Philetaerus (fourth century B.C.) and Poliochus (Athenaeus, *Deipnosophistae* 313c, 559a). In his short list of the second products of each Greek city Antiphanes (ca. 388–311 B.C.) associates 'bedspreads' with Corinth (Athenaeus, *Deipnosophistae* 27d). Plato (ca. 429–347 B.C.) used *korinthia koré*, "a Corinthian girl," to mean prostitute (*Republic* 404d). The dates of these authors should be noted because there are no citations from later periods. Such language was in fashion only in the fourth century B.C. There is no evidence that it was current in the first century A.D.
> (Murphy-O'Connor 2002: 56–7)

What Murphy-O'Connor describes in a concise way here was the image of Corinth. Strabo was probably influenced by this reputation of Corinth. Although Murphy-O'Connor notes that most of these sources are from the fourth century BCE, he points out that Plutarch too describes Corinth as having "a great army of prostitutes" (Plutarch, *Moralia*, 768a) (Murphy-O'Connor 2002: 57).

While Murphy-O'Connor says that "the sacred prostitution was common in the east," Stephanie Budin has recently argued that the whole idea of sacred prostitution in antiquity is a myth, propagated by ancient authors such as Herodotus and Strabo. "Sacred prostitution never existed in the ancient Near East or Mediterranean," Budin insists (Budin 2008: 1, see also 2009). She suspects that Strabo himself probably did not even know of this practice (Budin 2009: 198), but relied on rumors about it. Examining Strabo's use of words, such as *hierodule*, *hiera*, and *hiera sornata*, Budin argues that they "refer to sacrally manumitted slaves or individuals under the authority of a deity," and that "there were no sacred prostitutes in Corinth, or Comana, or Erfx. There were simply women protected by a goddess of love" (Budin 2009: 217–18).

In her work on erotic geography and Corinth as a place in Greece that ancient writers eroticized, classicist Kate Gilhuly highlights Strabo's reference to there being more than a thousand temple slaves in the temple of Aphrodite, Gilhuly argues that the association of Corinth with sexual perversion is actually a political problem, a product of anti-Corinth rhetoric—much like Trump's anti-immigrant rhetoric. Drawing on Benedict Anderson's conception of the imagined community, Gilhuly says:

> While there is no doubt that a culture of prostitution flourished in ancient Corinth, the pervasive association of Corinth with courtesans in Athenian representations (and those, like Strabo's, that are influenced by them) suggests that the notion of Corinth as a place of prostitution was significant as a discourse as well as a reality.
>
> (Gilhuly 2017: 11)

As a city of vibrant economic and cultural activities thanks to its geographically strategic position, Corinth itself had "a well-developed hospitality industry"—a hospitable space for visitors and those passing through. Because of that, Gilhuly argues, "The ability of the Corinthians to make the most of their geographic location is often given sexual parameters" (Gilhuly 2017: 14). It is through such "erotizing of geography" that ancient writers often linked Corinth to sexual passion and the sex trade.

All of this is to suggest that we understand this negative reputation of the Corinthians as a stereotypical and essentialist discourse that reduces a group of people into a single quality or essence. Another example of this is the English-language expression "to go Dutch," meaning not only to split a tab but often to be stingy, cheap. It stereotypes a group of people. It is a racist insult against the Dutch.

"Some Guy" (τινα)

Paul seems to tap into this negative stereotype of the Corinthians and use it as a weapon to rebuke them. After he deals with the messiness of the rejection of his authority in chapters 1 through 4, he threatens to come after them with a stick and beat them (4:21). Then, in chapter 5, Paul jumps to another rumor or stereotype that he heard about them. He states:

> It is actually reported (ἀκούεται) that there is sexual immorality (πορνεία) among you, and of a kind that is not found even among pagans (τά ἔθνη); for a man is living with his father's wife (γυναῖκά τινα τοῦ πατρὸς ἔχειν).

And you are arrogant! Should you not rather have mourned, so that he who has done this would have been removed from among you?

(5:1-2)

Important to note here is that Paul declares that he heard (ἀκούεται—it is heard/reported) this claim, presumably again from Chloe's people, that there is πορνεία among the Corinthians. He heard. It was reported to him. In short, he does not have direct knowledge of the case. He is dealing with secondhand information, a report, a *rumor*. And according to the report or rumor, "some man (τινα) is having his father's woman/wife." Before we talk about the sexualization and ethnicization of the Corinthian body, we should first examine this rumor.

We have no way of verifying whether this rumor is true or not. It is a rumor and ought to be treated as such. Paul apparently was not happy at all. Because we know that he felt quite threatened by the opposition to him from among the Corinthians, or more precisely from *some* Corinthians (4:18), his strong reaction to this rumor is understandable. He seems to say, "How dare you reject me? Take a look at yourselves! I heard that some bad things are happening among you!"

Because it is secondhand information, Paul himself might not have a clear idea of the precise situation in Corinth. His statement is, at best, vague. The use of "some guy" (τινα) is an indication of the vagueness of Paul's accusation. Who is this "some man," this τινα? We do not know. Paul does not name him. The use of τινα demonstrates that the man seems to be a random, nameless person from among the Corinthians—a stereotype. Paul often uses random person(s) in 1 Corinthians to make his point. A few verses prior to this statement he said that "some guys" (τινες) think that he is not coming to them (14:16). Who are these "some guys"? Just like τινα here, we do not know. He said in 3:4, that "some guy" (τις) says "I belong to Paul" and "another guy" (ἕτερος) says "I belong to Apollos." But who are these people? Again, we do not know. In 10:27-28, Paul imagines eating with unbelievers and "some guy" (τις) saying to them that the food they are now eating had been offered in sacrifice, and that they should not eat it. Who is this guy? We do not know. When Paul discusses the issue of tongue(s), he imagines "some unbeliever or outsider" (τις ἄπιστος ἢ ἰδιώτης) coming to their gathering. But who is this person? Again, we do not know.

Does Paul himself know who this "some guy" is? He probably does not. He likely heard about something vaguely sexual done by some man in Corinth and wrote a statement using this indefinite subject: τινα, some guy. While many Bible commentators skip over the significance of this indefinite pronoun in Paul's overall rhetoric, Joshua Reno argues that the choice of the word τινα instead of ἄνθρωπον or ἄνδρα or υἱόν or ἕνα ὑμῶν is "correctly designated as intentionally out of focus." Reno insists further, "Paul obscures the offender; he is not Paul's primary concern" (Reno 2016: 834).

While Reno is correct that the use of τινα demonstrates an "out of focus" expression, I do not think that Paul intentionally obscures the offender, for he seems to have no reason to do that. To my mind, it is much more likely that he does not know who the offender is. He is an imagined figure.

Perhaps the Corinthians asked Paul: "Who are you talking about? Who is this guy?" And Paul might have responded: "I don't know. All I heard is that some guy is having sex with his father's wife." This is akin to Trump's indefinite expression of "a lot of people are saying … " (see Johnson 2023). Does Trump even know who these people are—even one of them? Very likely not. He merely imagines them. Paul likewise merely imagines this guy.

In any case, this unknown guy is clearly a bad guy who represents what has gone wrong in this community. He is "the primary antagonist" (Reno 2018: 506) in Paul's narrative. Paul is clearly upset and Fitzmyer is not at all wrong to state that he "addresses it with even harsher terms than those he used in chaps. 1–4" (Fitzmyer 2008: 229). We will see later how harsh his language really is.

Those who study language know that *polyphony* is embedded in every linguistic expression—meaning that a multiplicity of meanings, and thus ambivalence and vagueness, is inherently normal in language. A word, a sentence, a paragraph, a writing, can have multiple significations. However, Paul's ambiguity is not caused merely by the imprecision of his language. It is also the result of his lack of firsthand knowledge of the situation. This inevitably adds a different significance to the ambiguity of his language. "Whatever the case, Paul nowhere makes explicit his understanding of this relationship," Renno notes (Reno 2016: 839). Is it possible that Paul does not make his understanding clear because he himself has no idea what exactly was going on? Yes. He heard from other people about this matter. He did not witness it himself. Is the report reliable? Has he substantiated it? Given the seriousness of his charge and response to it, those questions are worth asking. Scholars are often so busy exegeting every word of this rumor that, ironically, they overlook that it *is* a rumor.

"Having the Father's Wife"

Like the expression "some guy" discussed above, the exact crime that he is alleged to have been committed is also at best vague. In Greek, the expression "γυναῖκά τινα τοῦ πατρὸς ἔχειν" (some guy is having the father's wife/woman) is open to multiple possibilities. A few questions need to be asked. First, what does the verb "to have" mean here? What is the precise sense that Paul is conveying here? The verb "to have" (ἔχειν) is often used for "to be married" (see Mt. 1:18; 14:4; Lk. 20:28; 1 Cor. 7:12, 29), or to have sex (1 Cor. 7:2; Rom. 9:10). Is Paul referring to sexual activity or a marital commitment? In other words, is Paul taking about this man having sex with his father's wife (a sexual encounter) or of marrying her? Although they are related, they are two different things. The word "to have" is vague enough to imply both sexual and permanent relationship, although many scholars suspect the latter rather than the former. It is not clear to what exactly Paul is referring.

Second, what is the status of this woman in relationship to the son and the father? Is she his own mother or stepmother, or is she the father's concubine? If she is his mother, Paul could simply have used the word "mother" (μήτηρ) instead of "the father's wife" (Collins 1999: 209). Most scholars today would likely understand this as a relationship with a stepmother (Conzelmann 1975: 96; Fee 1988: 200; Harris 1991: 4; Blomberg 1995: 104; Witherington III 1995: 156; Collins 1999: 209). The argument that this is a stepmother can be traced all the way back to Chrysostom (*Homilies*, 1 Cor. 5). If she is a stepmother, why doesn't Paul make that clear by using the term μητρυιά—although Reno points out that this is not a "technical term"? (Reno 2016: 833). Still, if Paul had wanted to be more precise and avoid ambiguity, he could have used it.

Against the grain of scholarship that understands the father's wife as a stepmother, Craig Steven de Vos argues that if this is an incest situation, the couple would have been stoned to death. The fact that they could escape such a violent response demonstrates or at least suggests that she is probably in a different kind of relationship with the father. De Vos suggests that she is a concubine because "such a relationship ... provided the man with a sexual relationship without complications, while the woman normally gained a better standard of living than she could have otherwise expected" (Vos 1998: 111). Overall, this is a compelling argument. However, the textual basis of this theory is as weak as the stepmother theory. Paul does not seem to be at all interested in making things clear.

Third, is the father still alive? That also is not clear, but scholarly speculation abounds. Conzelmann, for example, insists that the father is still alive and that he has divorced the woman (Conzelmann 1975: 96). Although Gerald Harris is open to the possibility that the father is still alive and has been divorced, he likewise thinks that "the man may have married his deceased father's widow"—noting also that the truth is hard to discern (Harris 1991: 4). Again, Paul's statement is vague enough that it is not possible to know to what exactly he is referring. As Simon Kistenmaker puts it, "Paul fails to point out whether the father of this church member has passed away" (Kistemaker 1992: 36).

Fourth, is this a case of incest? Many scholars think so (Collins 1980; Zaas 1984; Harris 1991; Rosner 1994, 1998, 1998; Witherington III 1995: 156; Goulder 1999; McNamara 2010; May 2004: 58). The title that the NIV gives to 1 Corinthians 5 is "Dealing with a Case of Incest." Yet Paul nowhere uses the term "incestuous man." In order to make the case that this man is involved in an incestuous relationship, one first has to make clear what exactly is his relationship with the father's wife. Typically, scholars would point to Deuteronomy 27:20 and Leviticus. 20:11, *inter alia*, to make the case that this is an incestuous relationship between a son and a stepmother. However, as Reno has demonstrated that "kin circumlocutions" (like "the father's wife") are relatively common expression in Greek, found also in Homer, Herodotus, Polybius, etc. (Reno 2016: 830), he argues that "Paul's use of γυνή τοῦ πατρός, therefore, need not be restricted by insisting on an oblique septuagintal echo" (Reno 2016: 832). Challenging the idea that this is an incestuous relationship, Reno argues that the relationship between a man and a stepmother in ancient Greco-Roman literature is often seen simply as an example of adultery (μοιχεία), rather than of incest. But why doesn't Paul use the term μοιχεία? Instead, Paul uses a very vague term πορνεία, which I discuss further below.

Porneia

Paul makes all these vague descriptions of a relationship between a certain man and his father's woman/wife with one vague word: πορνεία (5:1). This word is surely key to unlocking what exactly was happening in Corinth, in what exactly this random guy was engaging. However, the problem is that the word *porneia* is one of those vague words that Paul has chosen to use. English speakers might immediately think they know what it means simply because it has an English cognate: porn. Yet the word "porn" in English refers mainly to sexually explicit images and videos. This was not at all the case in Paul's time. In fact, there are no instances in the ancient literature in which the word *porneia* refers to images that arouse sexual desire.

Scholars have spilled plentiful ink trying to explain the meaning of the word *porneia* here. In the particular context of 1 Corinthians 5:1, it is almost impossible to translate this word into English clearly. Why? Because, as we have seen, Paul does not paint a clear picture of what the case is all about. Many scholars simply decide to transliterate the term rather than translating it. In most English Bibles, however, the word *porneia* is translated "sexual immorality" (NRSV, NLT, NIV, ESV, BSB, and NKJV), though some translate it as "fornication" (KJB, ASV, ERV, Darby Bible). To translate it as "immoral" is a curious choice. As John Boswell points out, "Many English translators content themselves with the vague word 'immoral.' This is safe enough, since whatever else 'πορνεία' may be, it is certainly 'immoral,' but the term is misleadingly general" (Boswell 2015: 337). Reno similarly argues that "the English phrase '(sexual) immorality' ... is a nearly useless equivalent, given that it includes whatever sexual thoughts or actions the interpreter deems [to] fit" (Reno 2021: 164).

In ancient Greek literature, however, the term πορνεία is generally used to denote prostitution. (See an extensive survey in Wheeler-Reed and others 2018: 348–87.) The word πόρνη or πόρνος is a word for "prostitute." In the

Septuagint, the πορν- group appears within the range of meanings that includes prostitution (e.g., Gen. 38:24; Num. 14:33; Deut. 23:18; Hos. 1:2; 2:5; Micha) and idolatry (e.g., 1 Chron. 5:25; Jer. 2:20; Hos. 4:10, 12). These two concepts are clearly not separated from one another, as "idolatry is being condemned by metaphorical equation to prostitution" (Wheeler-Reed and others 2018: 387). This can be seen particularly in Hosea passages. Furthermore, the πορν- word group appears fifty-six times in the New Testament, and is translated in many different ways. The NRSV, for instance, translates *porneia* mostly as "fornication" (Mt. 15:19; Mk 7:21; Acts 15:20, 29; 21:25; 1 Cor. 6:13,18; Gal. 5:19, etc.), while in other places it translates it as "sexual immorality" (1 Cor. 5:1; 7:2; 2 Cor. 12:21), "illegitimate" children (ἐκ πορνείας οὐ γεγεννήμεθα; John 8:41), "unchastity" (Mt. 5:32; 19:9). The noun πόρνη (feminine) is typically translated as "prostitute" (Mt. 21:31,32; Lk. 15:30; 1 Cor. 6:15,16; Heb. 11:31; Jas 2:25), and only in the book of Revelation is it translated as "whore" (Rev. 17:1, 5,15,16; 19:2). The masculine version πόρνος, however, is rendered as "fornicator" (1 Cor. 6:9; Eph. 5:5; 1 Tim. 1:10; Heb. 13:4; Rev. 21:8; 22:15) and immoral person (1 Cor. 5:9; 5:10,11; Heb. 12:16). The verb πορνεύω those translations render as "to practice/commit fornication" (Rev. 2:14, 20;17:2; 18:9) and "to indulge in sexual immorality" (1 Cor. 10:8; Jd. 7). On the basis of this limited survey, one can see how the word *porneia* (and its cognates) can be and is understood and translated in many different ways, and that fornication still appears to be the dominant translation.

In English, the word "fornication" refers to a sexual relationship outside marriage. That is, when two people who are not married engage in sexual activities, they *fornicate*. Although Kyle Harper has argued quite forcefully that Christianity invented a new meaning for *porneia* as extramarital sex (Harper 2012, 2013)—a view that has been challenged by other scholars (see Glancy 2015; Wheeler-Reed and others 2018)—it is not really clear that it is to extramarital sex that Paul is referring, and this for two reasons: First, it is not clear whether the relationship between this random man and his father's wife is about sex itself or a long-term relationship—as we have explored above. Second, the appearance of the πορν- word group in 1 Corinthians 5–7 (5:1, 9; 6:13, 18; 7:2) is not clearly about sex outside marriage. In short, Paul uses this term rather freely without telling us precisely what he means by it.

Jimmy Hoke argues that the word πορνεία in 1 Corinthians 5:1 "does not seem to involve prostitutes, prostitution, or (necessarily) abuse. The text confirms that participants in Corinth's ἐκκλησία permitted sexual impulses that Paul deems nonnormative" (Hoke 2021: 323). Hoke's insight is important here, namely, that this word is probably not based on any actual reality, but on Paul's negative sentiment toward the Corinthians—like Trump's words with which we began. To understand what is going on in this chapter, we need to see Paul himself, rather than what this random man does. Moreover, *porneia* is a word of slander. Reno's 2021 study on *porneia* also shows that this word was widely used as an insult. "Moral opprobrium and rhetoric of disgust are parts of what it [*porn-*] communicates," he says (Reno 2021: 166). Paul is insulting the Corinthians. He is telling them that someone in their community is sexually disgusting and he is calling them out for doing nothing about it. So what does Paul want them to do?

Kill the Sinner!

By telling them "you are arrogant (πεφυσιωμένοι)!" (5:2), Paul shows that he is not happy with the way the Corinthians dealt with this sexually abhorrent man. This is the same word (φυσιόω) he uses in 1 Corinthians 4:18 when he accuses *some* Corinthians for being arrogant for saying that he is not coming back to Corinth. Here, in chapter 5, it is not just *some* Corinthians, but all of them that are arrogant. Paul expands his attack to include all Corinthians.

How does he want this situation to be addressed? There are two things he seems to think they should do, which they fail to do. First, he wants them to mourn, to lament, or grieve (πενθέω). Mourning is a reaction to a loss or death (2 Chron. 35:24; Mk 16:10; Rev. 18:11). By engaging in *porneia*, Paul has assumed that this person is dead and lost. He is no longer a member of the community. And precisely because of that, an appropriate response would be mourning (cf. 2 Cor. 12:21). But Paul does not see the Corinthians responding in this way. They instead allow this person to be part of them. They tolerate his *porneia*. Paul perceives them as being too open to difference and as not seeing this man's presence as a threat.

Second, Paul's rhetoric takes a sharply forceful turn as he urges the Corinthians to remove this individual from their midst. The term "removal" likely refers to excommunication—distancing themselves from the man in question (5:2). A few verses later, however, Paul intensifies his instruction, stating, "You are to hand this man over to Satan for the destruction of the flesh, so that his spirit may be saved in the day of the Lord" (1 Cor. 5:5). What does it mean to hand someone over to Satan for the destruction of the flesh? This unsettling and violent language has posed a significant challenge for Pauline scholars, as it "appears to say something morally or theologically objectionable," as David Horrell aptly describes it. Laura Nasrallah's recent work on *defixiones* (curse tablets) found in Roman Corinth and Paul's statement on the destruction of the flesh here demonstrates quite convincingly that it should be seen as a curse. The language of "judgment" (κατεργάζομαι; 5:3b) in this first-century Roman context, according to Nasrallah, "had a local resonance of destruction and annihilation." (Nasrallah 2021: 361, 2024; Smith 2009) Paul wishes this person to be annihilated, destroyed. To put it more bluntly, Paul wants this person to be *physically* killed. This is a declaration of a death sentence. Paul appears to want this person to be killed, destroyed. As Kathy Gaca agrees, saying it is possible "that Paul aims to stir up zealots in the community to kill the man outright" (Gaca 2003: 140). Similarly, Conzelmann argues that the statement "can hardly mean anything else but death" (Conzelmann 1975: 97). In other words, Paul insists on more than just a social removal or disassociation. He demands the man's physical termination as well.

The overall tone in this discourse shows that Paul advocates for purity within the community by enforcing sameness, a common theme in his letters where moral and theological unity is seen as essential for the body of believers. In this context, the pursuit of purity becomes tied to the eradication of difference, which Paul sees as a threat to the communal integrity. This demand for purity, however, leads to the violent exclusion of those who do not conform to this standard. It becomes not merely a call for moral correction, but for the removal of anything—or anyone—perceived as corrupting. Paul's analogy of yeast drives this point home. "Do you not know that a little yeast leavens the whole batch of dough? Clean out the old yeast so that you may be a new batch, as you really are unleavened" (1 Cor. 5:6b-7). Yeast, often used in biblical literature as a symbol of impurity or sin, must be purged (Exod. 12:15-20; 23:18; Lev. 2:11; Deut. 16:3). As Craig Keener puts it, "Although leaven was originally a symbol of haste, sometimes Jewish teachers used it to symbolize evil" (Keener 2005: 50).

The image is one of contamination. Just as a small amount of yeast causes the entire dough to rise, so too does impurity threaten to infiltrate and corrupt the whole community. The call to remove the "old yeast" serves as a metaphor for eliminating moral deviation, ensuring that the community remains "unleavened" or pure. The switch from "a little yeast" to "the old yeast" is curious and significant. Initially, Paul points to a small, seemingly insignificant influence—a "little yeast"—suggesting that even the smallest transgressions can have widespread, damaging effects. But in shifting to "the old yeast," Paul evokes a deeper history of impurity, perhaps referring to ongoing, entrenched sin within the community that needs to be thoroughly removed. This language emphasizes the need for a radical cleansing, not just of minor influences but of long-standing practices or individuals that threaten the sanctity of the group.

In this context, Paul's call for purity can be understood not merely as a theological or ethical exhortation but as a form of social control, where difference or dissent is forcibly excised to preserve the homogeneity and integrity of the community. The metaphor of yeast thus functions as a warning against the dangers of allowing any deviation, advocating for a stringent approach to purity that demands the removal of all that is "old" and impure. This passage highlights the tension between unity and exclusion, where Paul's vision of a pure and unified body is achieved by eliminating those who do not conform to the prescribed standard.

Paul seems to be keenly aware that the Corinthians might question both his authority and his negative depictions of their behavior. As their founding apostle and spiritual leader, Paul's influence over the Corinthian community is undeniable. However, his physical absence from them allows room for doubt and criticism. The Corinthians might argue: "Paul, while we respect your authority and past guidance, you are not here. You do not live among us, and therefore, you are disconnected from the realities we face. You are unaware of what is truly happening within our community. How can you speak with such authority about our situation when you are not present to witness it yourself? How can you even call for us to curse and condemn this person? Your absence weakens your arguments."

Paul likely anticipates this challenge to his authority, knowing that his absence weakens his ability to monitor the situation closely and respond appropriately. The physical distance between Paul and the Corinthians leaves a gap that could be filled with misunderstandings or competing perspectives. His absence does not help his case. Perhaps anticipating these objections, Paul addresses the issue head-on, emphasizing the continuity of his authority despite his physical distance. He responds assertively, "For though absent in body, I am present in spirit; as if present I have already pronounced judgment in the name of the Lord Jesus on the man who does such a thing" (1 Cor. 5:3). By stating that he is "present in spirit," Paul asserts that his spiritual authority transcends the limitations of physical absence. His bond with the community is not severed by geographical distance.

In fact, Paul's spiritual presence is so powerful that he has already rendered judgment as though he were physically present. The phrase "in the name of the Lord Jesus" reinforces that Paul's authority comes not from his physical presence but from his relationship with Christ. His judgment is not based on personal opinion or proximity but is rooted in the divine authority granted to him as an apostle. This assertion reaffirms his right to guide and discipline the Corinthians, regardless of where he is.

Paul's claim to be "present in spirit" is also a strategic rhetorical move. It positions him as both a leader deeply involved in the spiritual life of the community and someone who sees beyond the surface-level issues that the Corinthians might raise. His absence may indeed provide an opening for critique, but Paul quickly closes that gap by emphasizing his spiritual authority and his capacity to pronounce judgment even from a distance. By invoking the name of the Lord Jesus, he further strengthens his argument, reminding the Corinthians that his judgment carries divine weight. Thus, Paul navigates the potential critique of his absence by asserting that, while physically removed, his spiritual authority remains intact. His leadership is not diminished by distance, and he continues to speak with the full weight of his apostolic office, backed by the authority of Christ himself. This response seeks to disarm any argument that his absence weakens his position or invalidates his critique of the Corinthians.

In Closing

Paul's rhetoric in 1 Corinthians, especially his insistence on the removal of individuals he deems morally corrupt, can be compared to the tactics employed by leaders like Donald Trump, who construct a dangerous "other" to galvanize their audience. Trump's portrayal of immigrants—often vague, undefined individuals—as rapists and criminals deliberately presents them as a threat that must be dealt with through removal and exclusion. In the same way, Paul's condemnation of a "some guy" in the Corinthian community, whose actions are reported through secondhand information, creates a sense of moral danger that he believes must be eliminated.

Both Paul and Trump are dealing with unnamed, vague figures—individuals they may not know personally but who become symbolic of what they deem to be larger problems. Paul portrays this unnamed person's sexual misconduct as a moral infection threatening the purity of the entire Corinthian community. His call for the removal of this person reflects his belief that their presence endangers the spiritual integrity of the church, much like Trump's rhetoric of building walls and expelling "bad hombres" reflects a belief in the necessity of removing allegedly dangerous elements from society to protect national identity.

In both cases, the "other" is someone who exists more as an idea or symbol than as a fully known individual. These vague figures embody all that is wrong or dangerous and must be dealt with for the greater good of the community or nation. Paul's language, like Trump's, taps into fear and the desire for purity. Removal of the "dangerous other" becomes the solution to the perceived threat, whether it is moral contamination or societal instability.

This strategy of othering reinforces authority. By identifying a dangerous "other" and calling for its removal, both Paul and Trump position themselves as protectors of their communities, ensuring that unity, purity, and security are maintained.

6

The Politics of Many Tongues

In March 2015, during the celebration of National Foreign Language week, a student named Dana at an upstate New York high school recited the US Pledge of Allegiance in Arabic. Dana explained that for her, "The point of reading it in another language is that it doesn't matter what language you speak ... America is defined by what you believe, not what you speak or how you look. I wanted everyone to see this so we could see that deep cultural divide" (Silverstein and Chan 2015). Caught by surprise, however, her act sparked a huge controversy. The school was immediately divided in half, according to Joan Carbone, the school's superintendent (Starnes 2015). As Dana recited the Pledge in Arabic, "many students reportedly shouted their disapproval ... and later complained on social media" ("US Pledge of Allegiance in Arabic Leads School to Apologise" 2015). Alex Krug, one of the students who was not happy with Dana for reciting the Pledge in Arabic told Time Warner Cable News: "It's the Pledge of Allegiance, we're saying it to the American flag. I think it should be said in English. It is foreign language week but we don't even offer Arabic in Pine Bush High School" (Sayegh 2025). Even though it was only performed by one student, an online magazine, Right Wing News, provocatively and incorrectly reported that the school "has forced kids to recite the Pledge in Arabic" (Warner 2015).

The controversy swept through the nation like wildfire. After receiving enormous pressure, especially from the residents in the district who had lost family members in the Afghanistan war, the school finally issued a public apology "to any students, staff or community members who found this activity offensive," while promising that from that point forward the Pledge of Allegiance "will only be recited in English as recommended by the Commissioner of Education" ("New York School Apologises for Reciting Pledge of Allegiance in Arabic," 2015),

This story reminds us that language is not merely a means of communication or of expressing one's ideas: language is also a cultural representation. As Ngũgĩ wa Thiong'o puts it, "Language, any language, has a dual character: it is both a means of communication and a carrier of culture" (Thiong'o 1986: 13). The clash of languages is an indicator of the clash of cultures. However, it is worth noting that when we examine the politics of language, the power imbalance also has to be seriously considered.

This controversy over the Pledge of Allegiance in Arabic highlights how deeply intertwined language and identity can be in shaping community dynamics. Just as the backlash to Dana's Arabic recitation revealed underlying cultural and political tensions in contemporary America, so too the early Christian community in Corinth wrestled with the politics of language. In both cases, language was more than a tool for communication: it was also a marker of inclusion, exclusion, and power. The dynamics of multilingualism in Roman Corinth provide a rich backdrop for understanding the tension Paul faced in managing the diverse voices within the early church.

In this chapter, we will look into precisely this linguistic struggle in 1 Corinthians. As a city that received many immigrants (see Chapter 2), Roman Corinth was culturally a rich city. Immigrants came and resided in this city. Former slaves originally came from diverse places were sent by Julius Caesar to Corinth to rebuild the city. It was also a crucial center for export-import activities in the Mediterranean world due to the two major ports that connected the city to Saronic and Corinthian Gulfs. They kept this city busy and full of merchants and visitors. The Isthmian games, a panhellenistic festival celebrated every two years to honor Poseidon, the god of the sea to whom a temple was built in the Isthmus, likewise brought many foreigners to Corinth. In Corinth, we can find specific names of immigrants like Alexas and Sarapias from Syria and Nicostratus from Sardis. A Roman woman named Junia Theodora (Ἰουνία Θεοδώρα) was honored for showing hospitality and receiving Lycian immigrants into her home. So Marcin N. Pawlak is correct that "the population of Roman Corinth was ethnically and socially diverse from the very beginning" (Pawlak 2013: 143).

Like the United States, in the Roman period the city of Corinth was rich in immigrants. The two dominant imperial languages in Corinth were Latin and Greek. This does not mean that other languages did not exist in addition to these imperial languages. The fact that many immigrants use English in Los Angeles, for instance, does not mean that their native languages do not exist. They exist but often are overpowered or sublimated by English. This was the case also for Roman Corinth. Consequently, it is not too difficult to imagine that when early Christians gathered for communal worship, they would speak in their own languages. Clearly F. C. Baur understood this when he stated, "In a trading city like Corinth, knowing a few languages other than Greek was certainly nothing unusual" (Baur 1830: 79). The dominance of Greek and Latin does not necessarily mean that other languages were absent. The sociolinguistic dynamic on the street of Roman Corinth was likely a lot richer than just Greek and Latin. A hint of it can be seen in 1 Corinthians 14, to which I now turn.

What Is "Speaking in Tongue(s)"?

To understand the language struggle in Corinth, we need to examine closely the phenomenon of speaking in tongue(s) in chapters 12 to 14. The noun *glossa* (tongue) in 1 Corinthians appears in singular and plural forms. Of fifty instances of the word *glossa/i* (tongue/s) in the New Testament, it appears twenty-one times in 1 Corinthians (four times in chapter 12, twice in chapter 13, and sixteen times in chapter 14). The combination of this word and *lalein* (to speak) only appears in chapter 14 (in vv. 2, 4, 5, 13, 23, 27). In most of the Septuagint, the Greek word *glossa* is used to translate the Hebrew word lāšôn (tongue) or *śāpâ* (lip). In some places, the reference is clearly to language rather than to the body part (see Gen. 10:5, 10, 31; Isa. 66:18; Jer. 5:15). A rare case where the combination of *glossa* and *lalein* appears is Isaiah 19:18, but there it clearly refers to the Canaanite language (πέντε πόλεις ἐν Αἰγύπτῳ λαλοῦσαι τῇ γλώσσῃ τῇ Χανανίτιδι—five cities in Egypt speaking in the Canaanite tongue/language). Again, even in the LXX, the phrase "speaking in a tongue" refers to a specific human language.

Biblical scholars have widely understood speaking in tongue(s), particularly in Corinth, to refer to ecstatic, unintelligible speech. In the words of Luke Timothy Johnson, *glossolalia* "is not a real language but an ecstatic utterance which takes the form of an ordered babbling" (Johnson 1998: 113). Some Pauline interpreters today see a parallel between *glossolalia* in the modern Pentecostal/Charismatic movement and the phenomenon of speaking in tongues in 1 Corinthians (Best 1975: 47; Williams 1975: 21; Keener 2005: 113; Yongnan 2013; Oyetade 2020). Especially in its connection to Acts 2, however, scholars tend to see them as two different phenomena. (See Walker 1906: 3–4.) Krister Stendahl, for instance, argues that the situation in Corinth with which Paul is dealing is a groaning-like (cf. Romans 8:26-27) *glossolalia* that consists of "words that have no meaning understandable to human beings." Acts 2 later narratively interprets this phenomenon as a linguistic experience. In Stendahl's words, the difference is "intelligible (Acts) and unintelligible (Paul) glossolalia" (Stendahl 1976: 117.) Thus, says Stendahl, we should not base our understanding of this phenomenon on Acts 2 (Stendahl 1976: 119). In other words, the true nature of this phenomenon can be found in 1 Corinthians, and Acts 2 is its theological distortion. Some other scholars, however, think that tongue(s) in both Acts 2 and 1 Corinthians are unintelligible ecstatic speech (Williams 1975; Johnson 1998: 111).

It is worth noting that the idea that tongue(s) is an ecstatic phenomenon did not appear until around the late eighteenth century. Before the nineteenth century, the consensus was that tongue(s) is a linguistic phenomenon. Tongue(s) refers to the miraculous ability to speak foreign languages. Tongue(s) as an ecstatic utterance was a newly invented interpretation by German biblical scholars in the nineteenth century who were profoundly influenced by the romantic and nationalist socialist context of Germany. Scholars such as Johann Herder, Friedrich Bleek, Hermann Olshausen, F. C. Baur, August Neander, and Heinrich Meyer insisted that tongue(s) should be understood as an explosion of the speaker's that causes their speech to become or revert to being unintelligible (see Tupamahu 2022.) This trend continues in many books on *glossolalia* in the twentieth century.

That being said, a case can be made from the text of 1 Corinthians that Paul is dealing with a multilingual situation here. First, the appearance of singular and plural *glossa* indicates that Paul is dealing with a language situation. It is quite hard to understand this play of singular and plural from the perspective of an ecstatic, unintelligible experience. Can we distinguish between the singularity of ecstatic speech and the plurality of ecstatic speeches? The answer is probably not. But if *glossa* is understood as language, we can see that Paul is playing with the singularity and plurality of languages.

Second, the word *glossa* is a common word in Greek for both language and a body part. Aristotle describes this twofold role of "tongue" as follows: '[Nature] uses the tongue [τῇ γλώττῃ] both for taste [τὴν γεῦσιν] and for articulation [τὴν διάλεκτον], of which taste is essential to life (and consequently belongs to more species), and articulate speech is an aid to living well' (Aristotle, *On the Soul,* 2.420b). The statement "εὐχαριστῶ τῷ θεῷ, πάντων ὑμῶν μᾶλλον γλώσσαις λαλῶ" (1 Cor. 14:18) can therefore be read as "I give thanks to God, I speak in more languages than all of you." Paul is not "boasting" that he has more spiritual experience than the Corinthians, but rather that he knows more languages than them. Furthermore, Paul's quotation of Isaiah 28:11 that God speaks in the lips of foreigners (ἐν χείλεσιν ἑτέρων) and in foreign languages (ἐν ἑτερογλώσσοις) could be understood to refer quite simply to languages other than one's mother tongue, instead of to mystical or spiritual speeches. This phenomenon should, therefore, be called *heteroglossia* (i.e., foreign/other languages).

Third, the often-quoted textual basis for the idea that tongue(s) is not language but an unintelligible utterance is 1 Corinthians 14:2. In English, this text reads: "For those who speak in a tongue do not speak to other people but to God, for no one understands them, since they are speaking mysteries in the Spirit." This statement can be easily read as the expression of an unintelligible speech on the part of the speaker and the hearer. The utterance itself is unintelligible. However, if we look closer, this might not be the case. The English expression "for no one understands them" comes from "οὐδεὶς γὰρ ἀκούει" in Greek, which can be translated as "for no one *hears*." It is clear that the unintelligibility of tongue(s) is only on the listener's part and not the speaker's. In other words, it is a one-sided unintelligibility. This situation can be understood as a foreign language. Although the language is completely intelligible, the listener cannot understand it.

More can be said about the linguistic nature of this phenomenon. The point is that when these early followers of Jesus got together, they would obviously speak their own native languages. Paul found this multilingual coexistence chaotic, and 1 Corinthians 12–14 is his effort to restore (linguistic) order in this community. He states his discursive goal is clearly in 14:40, namely that "all things should be done decently and in order." So, for Paul, tongue(s) is indecent and disordered. Before we discuss how Paul brings order and decency back to this community, a few words need to be said about πνευματικός and Paul's claim of authority over this community.

Pneumatikos

Paul's opening line in 12:1 frames the entire discussions in chapters 12 to 14. He writes, "Περὶ δὲ τῶν πνευματικῶν" (concerning spiritual persons/things). The genitive "τῶν πνευματικῶν" can be a neuter or masculine substantive adjective. The two are exactly the same in Greek. So the phrase can be translated as either the spiritual persons (masculine) or the spiritual things/ matters (neuter). Many English Bibles translate it as "spiritual *gifts*" (ESV, NASB, Amplified Bible, NKJV, ASV, NRSV), while some others render it as "spiritual things" (Literal Standard Version, World English Bible, New Heart English Bible) or "the gifts of the Spirit" (NIV), or "the special abilities the Spirit gives us" (NLT). Scholars are also divided on this issue.

The other appearances in 1 Corinthians point to both possibilities. In 2:13, for instance, Paul talks about "explaining spiritual things to spiritual people" (πνευματικοῖς πνευματικὰ συγκρίνοντες). Notice that he uses both masculine and neuter cases of the adjective πνευματικός in the same sentence. In other places, Paul uses it in both senses: spiritual person (ὁ πνευματικὸς) in 2:15, spiritual persons (πνευματικοῖς) in 3:1, spiritual things (τὰ πνευματικά) in 9:11, spiritual things (τὰ πνευματικά) in v 14:1, and a spiritual person (πνευματικός) in 14:37. The immediate context in chapter 14 seems to point to both possibilities (41:1 and 37). In short, Paul doesn't exclude either possibility (cf. Thiselton 2013: 910).

Beyond whether Paul refers to spiritual things/gifts or people, the question is why Paul frames his discussion in chapters 12 to 14 in this way? He sandwiches the discussion in chapters 12 to 14 with πνευματικός. He opens with τῶν πνευματικῶν (12:1) and closes with πνευματικός (14:37). Right before he discusses tongue(s) and prophecy, in 14:1 he again drops the word τὰ πνευματικά (spiritual things). These are important markers throughout chapters 12 and 14. But why does he do it? We get a hint from 1 Corinthians 14:37 where he says: "Anyone who thinks that he/she is a prophet or a spiritual person (προφήτης ... ἢ πνευματικός), must acknowledge that what I am writing to you is a command of the Lord." Here, Paul argues that someone who calls themselves a spiritual person has to acknowledge his divine authority and that everything that he writes is a command from

Jesus himself. Paul often appeals to divine authority to build his personal credibility amid sharp opposition (cf. Gal. 1:11-12).

One must understand this statement in light of his struggle with this community in 1 Corinthians 1–4, as discussed in the earlier chapters of this book. His statement in 2:13 provides an important hint for us to understand what he meant by πνευματικά. He begins his sentence with "ἃ ... λαλοῦμεν" (the things that we are saying). The neuter plural relative pronoun ἃ (the things/matters) he then elaborates further in that sentence as πνευματικά. The things that Paul is saying are spiritual things because their source is the Spirit. Therefore, those who understand them are πνευματικοί. This is where the connection between those two understandings discussed above lies. The point is obvious: spiritual people will accept the things that he writes. He then makes a sharp contrast between those who are spiritual (πνευματικοῖς) and the people of flesh (σάρκινοι) (2:12-16). If they understand and accept what Paul is saying, they are spiritual people. If they don't, then they are the people of flesh (σάρκινοι) and infants (νηπίοι) (see 1 Cor. 3:1). So, by framing his discussion in chapters 12 to 14 in terms of spiritual things/people, Paul once more appeals to divine authority to support his concerns and ideas about how things should be.

How to Deal with Differences?

We can think of everything that Paul says in chapters 12 to 13 as his way to build his case for ordering the use of foreign languages in this community in chapter 14. Chapters 12 to 13, therefore, serve as a preparation for his more specific critique of tongue(s) speakers. Since the necessity of the social order usually arises from the clashes of differences, chapters 12 to 13 give us some interesting insights into how Paul thinks of differences and multiplicities. Acknowledging that differences do exist in the church, Paul offers a few frameworks to make sense of them.

Confessional Framework (12:1-3)

Here Paul presents a twofold confessional criterion of the authenticity of all spiritual activities: (1) negatively, no cursing Jesus, and (2) positively, acknowledging the lordship of Jesus (12:3). The question is: Do any followers of Jesus in Corinth curse Jesus or deny the lordship of Jesus? We do not know. Paul never returns to these two criteria in the rest of chapters 12 to 14. Even in chapter 14, there is no hint that anyone in Corinth is doing either of these things. So why does Paul say this at the beginning of chapter 12? The only hint we can see is his insistence in 1 Corinthians 14:37 that the spiritual person should acknowledge that everything he (Paul) says is the "command of the Lord." In this sense, the acknowledgment of the lordship of Jesus might be directly connected to Paul's claim of divine authority.

Theological Framework (12:4-11)

Paul then moves to explain the various gifts (διαιρέσεις χαρισμάτων) or various activities (διαιρέσεις ἐνεργημάτων) or various services (διαιρέσεις διακονιῶν) in Corinth (12:4). All these words (i.e., gifts, activities, services) seem to point to the same thing. It is puzzling that people often only focus on the first one, χαρισμάτων. Hans Conzelmann's suggestion that πνευματικῶν should be understood as a neuter adjective (and thus is about spiritual gifts) because it is directly related to χαρισμάτων is inaccurate (Conzelmann 1975: 204). Paul does not only use the word χαρισμάτων, but also διακονιῶν, and ἐνεργημάτων. The word διακονιῶν is a feminine noun, so making a connection only to χαρισμάτων is rather an arbitrary interpretative move. The English expression "spiritual gifts" is largely based on this arbitrary connection between πνευματικῶν and χαρισμάτων.

That being said, Paul argues that all the activities in the church come from a divine source: i.e., the same Spirit, the same Lord, and the same God (see 1 Cor. 12:4-6). He then lists all these activities (or the "manifestation of the Spirit"—v. 7). Those are the word of wisdom (λόγος σοφίας), the word of knowledge (λόγος γνώσεως), faith (πίστις), the gifts of healings (χαρίσματα ἰαμάτων), the activities of powers (ἐνεργήματα δυνάμεων), prophecy (προφητεία), discernment of spirits (διακρίσεις πνευμάτων), and kind of languages (γένη γλωσσῶν), translation of languages (ἑρμηνεία γλωσσῶν). As Gordon Fee has pointed out, these are not an exhaustive nor ordered list of all the activities in the church (Fee 1980: 9). The function of this list in the larger context of 1 Corinthians 12–14 is to show that tongue(s) is just one of the activities in the church. There are many others too! All of them originate from the Spirit (12:11).

Social Body Framework (12:12-31)

The third framework is a social body analogy in 12:12-31. The human "body" is a common imagery in the Greco-Roman literature to explain human relations. What Paul does here is not new. This analogy is his effort to construct unity or oneness around Christ (and Spirit) to make sense of the diverse parts of the body. A *single* body consists of *many* parts (12:12). Each part is dependent on the others (12:14-26), and thus none is more important than the other. Paul concludes that everyone is a member of the body of Christ (12:27).

Right after he lays out this analogy, Paul presents another list of gifts/ activities: apostles, prophets, teachers, powers (δυνάμεις), gifts of healings (χαρίσματα ἰαμάτων), helps, administrations, kind of languages (γένη γλωσσῶν). Notice that there are some differences and similarities between this and the other list earlier (12:8-10), among them: (1) Apostles, prophets, teachers, help, and administrators are absent from the previous list; (2) powers are listed without ἐνεργήματα in this list; and (3) there is no "translation of tongues" in this list. Despite these differences, we can see that both lists include powers, gifts of healings, and kind of languages. Again, Paul seems to create a random list to show the diversity of activities in the church. These lists function are not exhaustive but exemplary. Paul then closes his argument with a series of rhetorical questions that require a "no" answer: "Are all apostles? Are all prophets? Are all teachers? Do all work miracles? Do all possess gifts of healing? Do all speak in languages? Do all translate?" (12:29-30). His point is that diversity is inevitable, and that every community has diverse gifts/activities.

Beyond that, it is interesting to note how Paul adds translation to this string of questions though he does not place it in the second list. There are three things to say about this appearance of translation. First, it shows that the two lists of gifts/activities in verses 8-10 and verse 28 are not rigid. Second, they serve a rhetorical purpose to show that the church consists of diverse people with diverse activities. Third, the placement of tongues and translation of tongues at the end of this string of questions must be intentional—to prepare his readers for what's coming in chapter 14.

The Love Framework (13:1-13)

Lastly, Paul provides another framework for dealing with diversity in the church, calling it "an excellent way" (12:31). Love, for Paul, must ground or be the basis of all the diverse activities in the church. He opens the conversation with an interesting statement on languages. He says, "If I speak in the languages of humans, even of angels (Ἐὰν ταῖς γλώσσαις τῶν ἀνθρώπων λαλῶ καὶ τῶν ἀγγέλων), but if I do not have love, I become a noisy gong or a clanging cymbal" (13:1). Many scholars point to this verse and argue that tongue(s) is an angelic language, or that at least Paul or the Corinthians viewed tongue(s) as the language(s) of angels. Dale Martin, for instance, argues that "Paul's statement about 'tongues of men' in 1 Cor. 13 is in opposition to 'tongues of angels.' The latter refers to glossolalia and the former to normal speech" (Martin 1991: 559, n. 23; see also Johanson 1979: 253; Poirier 2010). Besides Martin's problematic analysis of glossolalia based on a vague category of "status" (which has been criticized by Steve Friesen, as discussed on chapter 4), his insistence that there is no indication in 1 Corinthians that the tongues phenomenon is a linguistic experience is not true (see my discussion in Tupamahu 2022). Contrary to Martin, Paul here is not contrasting human language and angelic language he is using typical hyperbolic rhetoric to show that *any* language, *even* the angelic ones, is useless without love. The point is that love is more important than the diversity of languages. Also, Paul never mentions tongues of angels in other parts of 1 Corinthians or in other letters.

This exaggeration can be seen in the next verses in which Paul talks about prophecy, the understanding of *all* mysteries and *all* knowledge, and having *all* faith to remove mountains (13:2). Who has these capacities in their *totality*? No one. So why does Paul list them? Because he is exaggerating them. Again, this is not a true picture of reality but an exaggerated rhetoric. He aims to demonstrate that, just like languages, love is above all other gifts/activities in the church. The same is true of people who give away all their possessions, sacrifice their bodies [for others], and boast about it. Without love, they don't accomplish anything. (13:3) Love is above all these marvelous things.

But what is love? Paul provides a list of positive qualities of love. "Love is patient; love is kind; love is not envious or boastful or arrogant or rude. It does not insist on its own way; it is not irritable or resentful; it does not rejoice in wrongdoing, but rejoices in the truth. It bears all things, believes all things, hopes all things, endures all things" (13:4-7), He then compares love with three other activities: prophecies, tongues, and knowledge. All of them will fade away and cease. Love does not. The reason they will fade away and end, for Paul, is because they are partial (ἐκ μέρους) (13:9) and childish things (τὰ τοῦ νηπίου) (3:11).

To explain the partiality of all these gifts further, he uses two analogies: that of an infant and that of a mirror. The analogy of the infant (νήπιος) points to the inability to understand or reason like an adult man (ἀνήρ). Once adulthood is reached, according to Paul, infancy is left behind. The word νήπιος (infant) might evoke for the Corinthians Paul calling them infants earlier, in 3:1. Furthermore, the partiality is like seeing through a mirror in a puzzling way. The word "puzzling" in Greek is αἴνιγμα, which is the root of the word "enigma" in English. The mirror gives an enigmatic picture of reality. The problem is not the mirror itself but the act of seeing through a mirror. Seeing through a mirror will not give us a true picture of reality. It's a reflection, and any reflection is enigmatic or puzzling. Therefore, Paul looks into the future to see things face to face, implying a future full and direct knowledge (13:12). He closes this section on love with a reaffirmation of the importance of love: "And now faith, hope, and love abide, these three; and the greatest of these is love."

The Silencing of Foreign Languages

After presenting these four frameworks, Paul immediately criticizes the people who speak many languages in Corinth: the tongue(s) speakers. We have seen that a case can be made for the phenomenon of tongue(s) being because of the multilingual situation in the Corinthian church. Tongue(s) speakers provide a practical test to Paul's theoretical discussion on unity and diversity in chapters 12 to 13. This is where the rubber meets the road. How does Paul deal with this multilingual situation? Paul's overall argument in Chapter 14 is that because one cannot understand languages that are foreign to one, they should not be expressed in public unless they are also translated. If there is no translator, the foreign language speaker should be silent. This is his core thesis.

We can observe a few things about Paul's dealing with foreign languages in Corinth. First, he makes a sharp distinction between prophecy and tongue(s). Paul wants the Corinthians to prophesy (14:1). This is quite an odd encouragement in light of what he said previously—that not all can be prophets (12:29). That said, it seems that chapter 14 is not about the *content*, but the *form* of the prophecy. It is about *how* the message is communicated. He says, "One who prophesies is greater than one who speaks in tongues, unless someone interprets, so that the church may be built up" (14:5). For Paul, prophecy is greater because it builds up the church (see 14:4). If speech in tongues is translated, it will likewise build up the church. In other words, prophecy and tongue(s) become equal when tongue(s) is translated. The only distinction between tongue(s) and prophecy in this context is intelligibility. This means that if tongue(s) is a phenomenon of foreign languages, then prophecy is utterance in the dominant language. The distinction between these two activities is thoroughly linguistic. By saying that prophecy is greater than tongue(s), Paul constructs a stratification of language. Any speech that is understandable by the dominant group is greater or better than foreign minoritized languages.

Second, Paul believes that using foreign languages in public spaces is a useless practice. It is better, he argues, to speak five words that people can understand than a thousand foreign words (1 Cor. 14:9). "Now, brothers and sisters, if I come to you speaking in tongues (or foreign languages), how will I benefit you unless I speak to you in some revelation or knowledge or prophecy or teaching?" The word "to benefit" (ὠφελέω) can also mean "to be of use to" or "to be useful." Foreign languages are useless for revelation, prophecy, or teaching. Why? Paul presents an analogy to musical instruments as an argument for the uselessness of foreign languages. Flute, harp, or trumpet, Paul explains, have to produce the distinct voice or tone of the flute, harp, or trumpet, so that people know that it is flute, harp, or trumpet that is being played. Paul's point of the analogy is quite simple: "How will anyone know what is being said?" (14:9) These sounds are not understandable.

Third, if they speak in foreign languages, outsiders might think they are mad. The argument against the usefulness of foreign languages is further intensified in 1 Corinthians 14:13, where Paul envisions the presence of ἰδιῶται (private individuals, uneducated people, or those who do not know other languages) in their gathering. The conditional construction of ἐάν plus the subjunctive verb indicates that this is not a statement of fact, but rather a scenario Paul imagines. Paul strategically creates these hypothetical actors to emphasize his belief that speaking in foreign languages is ineffective and leads only to confusion. When these ἰδιῶται enter a church gathering and observe the congregation speaking in foreign languages, Paul insists that they might conclude the people in the church are out of their minds (mad or crazy).

Fourth, when foreign languages are spoken in the church gathering, Paul insists further that these languages be accompanied by translation. He even wants the person who speaks in a foreign language to pray so that he/she is able to translate it thoroughly (4:13 διερμηνεύῃ). For Paul, foreign language has to be translated either by the speaker themselves or by some other persons. Similarly, he states in 14:27, "If anyone speaks in a foreign language (a tongue) followed by two or three other speakers, let one translate." Who is "one" here? It could be someone in the gathering or the speaker themselves. In the next sentence, Paul talks about the absence of a translator (διερμηνευτής). Foreign tongues speaking has to be accompanied by a translator/translation.

Fifth, if not translated, Paul forbids the use of foreign languages altogether. This is what he writes: "But if there is no translator, let them be silent in church and speak to themselves and to God." (1 Cor. 14:28) This is a clear command to forbid any performance of foreign languages in public gatherings. For Paul, the linguistic order in this community has to be structured around monolingualism. Only the dominant language that people can understand is allowed to be expressed. Other languages have to be silenced.

In connection with Paul's effort to regulate speaking in tongues, he introduces a sudden discussion on the silencing of women (1 Cor. 14:33b-36). The abruptness of the shift to this topic within the broader discussion has puzzled many scholars. What does the silencing of women have to do with speaking in tongues or foreign languages? Scholars have debated whether these verses were part of the original text of 1 Corinthians or whether they are later interpolations. If these verses are an interpolation, Paul would not be responsible for the directive to silence women; rather, some sexist or misogynistic scribes could have inserted it long after 1 Corinthians was written. Richard Hays, for example, argues: "The whole passage is much more coherent without these extraneous verses. Paul never told women to be silent in churches; this order is the work of a subsequent Christian generation" (Hays 2011: 157).

However, this position is difficult to maintain. First, no extant manuscripts omit these verses. While some ancient manuscripts place the passage after verse 40, this does not conclusively indicate that it is a later addition. The evidence for interpolation is insufficient. Moreover, as Elisabeth Schüssler Fiorenza has observed, both the discussions on speaking in tongues and women share the theme of "order" (Schüssler Fiorenza 1994: 230). Paul's treatment of both subjects may not be entirely separate, suggesting a continuity of thought regarding the proper ordering of the church community.

Another clue to the connection between these discussions is the use of the word "as" or "just like" (ὡς), a term often employed to indicate a parallel or analogy. Paul seems to draw an analogy between the silencing of women and the restriction on foreign languages (Tupamahu 2022). Just as women are not permitted to speak in churches, so too foreign languages are prohibited. For Paul, women are only allowed to speak at home to their husbands. This reflects a "subordination ideology" (Økland 2005: 202), similar to Paul's view on the relationship between tongues and prophecy. In this way, the silencing of women mirrors the silencing of tongues: speakers of foreign languages are feminized, with femininity being portrayed as a subordinated category. Women as well as foreign language speakers must be silent in the church.

What Would Have Been the Corinthians' Reaction?

The Corinthian tongue(s) speakers would likely have rejected Paul's command to silence them. They might have shared Paul's view that linguistic diversity is a gift from the Spirit (12:10), and thus, might have felt very frustrated and marginalized by Paul's insistence on monolingualism in public gatherings. If they saw their language as a crucial part of their identity and experience, they would likely have interpreted Paul's command to be silent as a personal and cultural affront, causing tension between them and those who supported Paul's stance.

The tongue(s) speakers might argue that even if Paul requires translation, translation itself is an impossibility. They would likely recognize that no translation can fully capture the meaning, context, and nuances embedded in the original language. As a result, the performance of foreign languages does not disappear completely in translation, because the act of speaking in those languages still conveys important cultural and social identities. The speakers might feel that the demand for translation reduces their linguistic expression to something more manageable for the dominant group, but that in doing so they might realize that it overlooks the deeper layers of meaning that are inherently untranslatable. They might argue that translation cannot adequately replace the original because much of what is expressed in a language—its cultural significance, its specific rhythms, and its subtleties—resists being conveyed in another language.

This could further frustrate them, as they might regard Paul's insistence on translation not only as a practical demand but as a fundamental misunderstanding of the nature of language itself. In this light, Paul's directive could be perceived as a form of control that erases the richness of their linguistic diversity, rather than a simple solution to the issue of intelligibility.

As for the Corinthian women, they might also resist Paul's command to remain silent in public gatherings. Just as the tongue(s) speakers could see Paul's instruction as a denial of their linguistic and cultural identity, so too the women in Corinth might interpret the demand for their silence as a denial of their participation and agency in the community. In a city like Corinth, where various social norms and cultural expectations were constantly being negotiated, many women might have felt that Paul's directive limited their role in the life of the church, confining them to the domestic sphere.

The women might also have questioned the consistency of Paul's stance, especially if they had previously been involved in public worship, prayer, or prophecy, as suggested by 1 Corinthians 11:5. For those who had already been active participants in the community, the sudden shift to silence would likely have felt like a regression, and they might have resisted what they saw as a reassertion of patriarchal control. Perhaps they argued that their voices were just as valuable and necessary for the building up of the church as the voices of men, and that silencing them based on gender was an unjust exclusion that mirrored broader societal hierarchies.

Furthermore, perhaps some women draw parallels between their own experience and that of the tongue(s) speakers. Both groups were being silenced for reasons of intelligibility or order, yet both could argue that their exclusion was more about maintaining control over who got to speak and be heard in the community. Like the tongue(s) speakers, the Corinthian women perhaps viewed Paul's directive not just as a practical measure for order but as a form of marginalization that reflected broader social inequalities.

In Closing

In the end, the politics of many tongues in the Corinthian church reveals a deep struggle over power, identity, and belonging. For Paul, the regulation of tongues and the silencing of women were ways to impose order on a diverse and often chaotic community. Yet these regulations also reflect broader patterns of exclusion that have continued throughout history, where dominant languages and voices suppress those deemed "other." Just as the controversy surrounding the Pledge of Allegiance in Arabic demonstrates, language remains a key site of cultural conflict, revealing the complexities of power and identity in any society. Examining these dynamics in 1 Corinthians invites us to consider how language continues to shape not only our religious communities but also our political and social worlds.

Conclusion

I wrote some parts of this book while on an airplane flying to London, UK. Sitting in the same seat for eight hours on a long-haul flight from Houston to London can be quite monotonous, so to break the boredom, I decided to download and watch season four of *Virgin River* on Netflix. In the second episode, Jack, the protagonist, is visited by his father, a professor who is deeply obsessed with his career—publishing, teaching, and living up to the standards of academia. Against his father's wishes, Jack had rejected the opportunity to attend UC Berkeley on a full scholarship, choosing instead to enlist in the Marines. This decision had caused a significant rift between father and son, and they hadn't spoken in years. As Jack recounts, "When I was growing up, my father insisted that I follow in his footsteps," describing the strained relationship caused by his father's rigid expectations.

Jack's story parallels Paul's relationship with the Corinthians in many ways. Just as Jack's father demands that his son follow the path he chose for him, Paul seems to demand that the Corinthians adhere to his teachings and moral standards. The father's expectation is that Jack will follow in his footsteps, become the person he envisioned, and live a life according to the father's ideals. Similarly, Paul exerts pressure on the Corinthians to follow his cultural and ethical direction, seeing himself as their guide, their authoritative parent. But just as Jack resisted his father's plan for him, the Corinthians appear to resist Paul's attempts to shape their community.

In a pivotal scene, Jack confronts his father on a porch overlooking a river, a metaphorical setting for the emotional distance between them. He tells his father, "Look, I know you don't approve of my choices, but that shouldn't mean that we can't have a civil conversation." Here, Jack tries to create a space for mutual respect, despite their differences, hoping for a relationship where disagreement doesn't have to lead to alienation. His father, however, seems bewildered by Jack's defiance and responds, "I just don't understand why you always have to go against the grain," lamenting that Jack hadn't taken the opportunity to go to Berkeley and follow the life path laid out for him. Jack, resolute in his decisions, says, "I'm living the life I want. I don't know why you can't understand that."

This dialog echoes the tensions between Paul and the Corinthians that we have explored throughout this book. Paul, like Jack's father, cannot seem to accept the Corinthians' decisions to chart their own course. As a "father," Paul's desire to protect and guide his "beloved children" is evident. He cares for them and feels responsible for their spiritual well-being. But like Jack, the Corinthians are asserting their independence, choosing paths that diverge from Paul's teachings. They seem to be saying, "There's more than one way to live a life," echoing Jack's words to his father. This sentiment captures the Corinthians' likely frustration with Paul's forceful imposition of his views.

The Corinthians might argue that Paul's way of life, while valid for him, is not the only one. There are multiple paths to spiritual maturity, moral integrity, and communal well-being. Paul's insistence that they follow his teachings exclusively—and the forceful rhetoric he uses to ensure compliance—seems to overlook the diversity of thought, experience, and belief within the community. His method of leadership, grounded in authority and strong admonitions, may feel heavy-handed to the Corinthians, who are trying to assert their autonomy.

Imposing his authority on the Corinthians through such strong, and at times even harsh, rhetoric appears counterproductive for maintaining leadership over this complex and dynamic community. Similar to how Jack's father's relentless demand for conformity only deepened the divide between them, Paul's authoritarian tone risks alienating the very community he seeks to lead. The Corinthians, like Jack, may be calling for understanding and respect for their choices, challenging Paul to recognize that there are different ways of embodying Christian life and discipleship. Paul's task, then, is to navigate the tension between his desire for authority and the Corinthians' desire for autonomy. Just as Jack's relationship with his father needed a shift from control to mutual respect, so Paul's relationship with the Corinthians might benefit from a similar transformation, recognizing that his way is not the only way and that true leadership involves guiding without dominating.

However, one might still wonder: Why is Paul so insistent on asserting his authority over this community? I offer a *possible* answer.

Money and Politics

Toward the very end of 1 Corinthians, Paul introduces the last occurrence of περὶ δὲ ("now concerning"), addressing a specific issue raised by the Corinthians, before offering final exhortations, greetings, and personal instructions. This transitional section marks the culmination of his theological discourses throughout the letter. Here, Paul shifts focus to a practical matter, yet one deeply intertwined with his theology and mission. He writes:

> Now concerning the collection for the saints: you should follow the directions I gave to the churches of Galatia. On the first day of every week, each of you is to put aside and save whatever extra you earn, so that collections need not be taken when I come. And when I arrive, I will send any whom you approve with letters to take your gift to Jerusalem. If it seems advisable that I should go also, they will accompany me."
> (1 Cor. 16:1-4)

This instruction reveals Paul's deep concern for the believers in Jerusalem, a community facing hardships. While Paul does not explicitly mention famine in this passage, the book of Acts refers to a famine during the reign of Claudius (Acts 11:28), which may have contributed to the needs in Jerusalem. Paul repeatedly addresses the collection for the Jerusalem saints in his other letters, most notably in 2 Corinthians 8-9, where he elaborates on the importance of generosity. Furthermore, in his letter to the Galatians, Paul recounts that during a visit to Jerusalem, the leaders of the church affirmed his mission to the Gentiles but requested one thing: "that we remember the poor, which was actually what I was eager to do" (Gal. 2:10). This commitment to aiding the poor in Jerusalem remained a priority for Paul throughout his ministry.

In Romans 15, Paul reveals his desire to visit the church in Rome on his way to Spain but notes that before doing so, he must first go to Jerusalem. He explains, "For Macedonia and Achaia have been pleased to share their resources with the poor among the saints in Jerusalem" (Rom. 15:26). Corinth, located in Achaia, played a vital role in this fundraising effort, demonstrating that Paul's collection campaign had achieved some success in this region.

A closer reading of 1 Corinthians 16:1-4 highlights the authoritative tone Paul uses in addressing this matter. Rather than offering a suggestion or a polite request, Paul issues a direct command, employing the imperative verb (ποιήσατε), rather than the more tentative hortatory subjunctive. The English translation, "you should follow the directions I gave to the churches of Galatia," softens this a bit. The Greek expression in verse 1 can be more accurately translated as: "Now concerning the collection for the saints, you do just as I commanded (διέταξα) the churches in Galatia." The use of the Greek verb διατάσσω (to direct, require, order, command) further strengthens the imperative tone.

What exactly is the command Paul gave to the Galatians? That on every first day of the week, i.e., Sunday (Thiselton 2013: 1321), they set aside whatever extra they have earned. In other words, "regular tiny deposits of money" (Barclay 2019: 91) are to be put aside before Paul's arrival. His rationale is noteworthy: "So that collections need not be taken when I come," he says. Paul seems to want to avoid a large, one-time collection upon his arrival, which could be burdensome for the Corinthians. Instead, by contributing small amounts each week, the sum would accumulate over time and grow into a significant amount without imposing sudden financial strain.

Because the amount collected is likely substantial, Paul emphasizes the need to send it with someone the Corinthians trust within their own community. He adds, "If it seems advisable that I should go also, they will accompany me," indicating his willingness to oversee the delivery personally if necessary. However, from his letter to the Romans, we know that while Paul allows others to deliver the collection, he is eager to ensure its safe arrival. This eagerness may reflect his need to demonstrate to the leaders in Jerusalem that he is following through on their request to "remember the poor" (Gal. 2:10).

Now, consider Paul's position: Could he have given them this command if they were not under his authority? Would they actually follow his instructions and set aside their income for the collection? Perhaps not. This might explain why Paul is so intent on reasserting his control and leadership over the Corinthians. The collection is not merely a matter of charity: it's a critical aspect of his ministry and identity as an apostle to the uncircumcised. For it to succeed, the Corinthians need to listen to and obey him. Furthermore, the fact that some in the Corinthian community were following other leaders would not help his cause. Their divided allegiances would undermine Paul's authority and his ability to secure the necessary support for the collection. Paul's insistence on their cooperation and unity, therefore, is driven not only by the practical necessity of securing the funds but also by the need to maintain his influence over a community that was key to his mission. Recognizing his authority is essential if his efforts are to be successful.

Knowing that "some" Corinthians were saying that Paul was not coming back (4:18), this would have directly affected their motivation to gather the collection. If they believed Paul was not returning, they would feel no urgency or obligation to follow through on his command. This skepticism about Paul's return undermined not only his authority but also the practical outcome of the collection itself. If they doubted his return, they might have disregarded the instruction to set aside funds weekly, as Paul had directed. This perhaps explains why Paul felt it necessary to reassert his leadership and stress the importance of the collection. Their refusal to gather the funds would not only reflect their lack of trust in Paul's word but also jeopardize his broader mission to support the Jerusalem community. Without their participation, the collection—central to Paul's ministry—could fail, affecting his standing as an apostle.

That said, this call for the Corinthians to contribute to the collection for the Jerusalem saints would likely have elicited a range of responses, reflecting the diversity within the Corinthian church. Some members, perhaps those who remained loyal to Paul and respected his authority, would have viewed this appeal as a natural extension of their shared Christian identity. For them, contributing to the needs of the Jerusalem community could have symbolized their unity with the broader church, affirming their solidarity with Jewish believers in Jerusalem. They may have seen this act of generosity as a practical expression of their faith, embodying the Christian principles of charity and care for the poor. These Corinthians might have followed Paul's instructions diligently, trusting in his leadership and recognizing the importance of supporting a church facing hardship.

However, others in the community may have reacted with skepticism or even resistance. Given the ongoing tensions between Paul and certain factions within the church, some Corinthians might have questioned why their resources should be directed to a distant community with which they had little personal connection. For these individuals, Paul's insistence on the collection might have felt like an imposition of authority, especially in light of the community's divisions and allegiances to other leaders. Furthermore, practical concerns about their own financial well-being or a desire to focus on the needs of the local community could have fueled reluctance to participate. This mixed reaction—ranging from enthusiastic support to outright defiance—highlights the complex dynamics Paul faced as he sought to maintain influence and foster unity within this diverse and independent church.

A Final Reflection

As you reach the end of this book, you may find yourself wondering: Where is the resolution to this situation? Everything remains open, conflicted, and unresolved. Yet, this very tension lies at the heart of Paul's relationship with the Corinthians—and, perhaps, at the core of all relationships between leaders and their communities. Rather than offering a clear victory or a neat resolution, Paul's interactions with the Corinthians reveal the ongoing complexity of leadership, authority, and community life. The unresolved nature of their conflict serves as a reminder that life in a community is rarely about arriving at definitive conclusions. Instead, it is a continuous negotiation of differences, a dynamic balance between guidance and independence, authority, and autonomy. As Homi Bhabha puts it, "The social articulation of difference, from the minority perspective, is a complex, on-going negotiation that seeks to authorize cultural hybridities that emerge in moments of historical transformation" (Bhabha 1994: 3).

In many ways, this unresolved tension reflects the realities of human relationships, both then and now. Just as Paul struggled to balance his role as a leader with the Corinthians' desire for self-determination, leaders today also face the challenge of offering direction while allowing room for growth. Perhaps the lack of resolution is not a failure but an invitation to embrace the complexities of life together—recognizing that the journey, like Paul's relationship with the Corinthians, is filled with moments of conflict, tension, and ultimately, transformation. The open-endedness of this situation reminds us that living in a community is not about enforcing uniformity, but about fostering spaces where diverse paths of life can coexist.

BIBLIOGRAPHY

Adams, Sean A. 2008. "Crucifixion in the Ancient World: A Response to L.L. Welborn," in *Paul's World*, ed. by Stanley E. Porter (Brill), pp. 111–29.
Adams, Sean A. 2012. "The Relationships of Paul and Luke: Luke, Paul's Letters, and the 'We' Passage of Acts," in *Paul and His Social Relations*, Pauline Studies, 7, ed. by Stanley E. Porter and Christopher D. Land (Leiden: Brill), pp. 125–42.
Ahmed, Sara. 1999. *Differences That Matter: Feminist Theory and Postmodernism* (Cambridge: Cambridge University Press).
Bakhtin, Mikhail Mikhailovich. 2004. *The Dialogic Imagination: Four Essays*, ed. by Michael Holquist, trans. by Michael Holquist and Caryl Emerson (Austin, TX: University of Texas Press).
Barclay, John M. G. 1958–2004. "Poverty in Pauline Studies: A Response to Steven Friesen," *Journal for the Study of the New Testament*, 26.3: 363–6.
Barclay, John M. G. 2019. "Paul and the Gift to Jerusalem: Overcoming the Problems of the Long-Distance Gift," in *Poverty in the Early Church and Today: A Conversation*, ed. by Steve Walton and Hannah Swithinbank (London: T&T Clark), pp. 88–97.
Barclay, William. 1962. *The Letter to the Romans* (Edinburgh: Saint Andrew Press).
Barrett, Charles Kingsley. 1964. "Christianity at Corinth," *Bulletin of the John Rylands Library*, 46.2: 269–97.
Barrett, C. K. 1971. "Paul's Opponents in II Corinthians," *New Testament Studies*, 17.3: 233–54.
Barrett, C. K. 2003. "Sectarian Diversity at Corinth," in *Paul and the Corinthians: Studies on a Community in Conflict : Essays in Honour of Margaret Thrall*, ed. by Trevor J. Burke and J. Keith Elliott (Leiden: Brill), pp. 287–302.
Baur, Ferdinand Christian. 1830. "Ueber Den Wahren Begriff Des Γλωσσαις Λαλειν, Mit Rückficht Auf Die Neuesten Untersuchungen Hierüber," in *Tübinger Zeitschrift Für Theologie*, ed. by Ferdinand Christian Baur and Friedrich Heinrich Kern (Tübingen: bei Ludw. Friedrich Fue'i.), pp. 75–133.
Baur, Ferdinand Christian. 1873. *Paul the Apostle of Jesus Christ: His Life and Works, His Epistles and Teachings* (Edinburgh: Williams and Norgate).
Baur, Ferdinand Christian. 2021. *The Christ Party in the Corinthian Community*, ed. by David Lincicum, trans. by Wayne Coppins, Christoph Heilig and Lucas Ogden (Atlanta, GA: SBL Press).
Best, Ernest. 1975. "The Interpretation of Tongues," *Scottish Journal of Theology*, 28.01: 45–62.
Bhabha, Homi K. 1994. *The Location of Culture* (New York: Routledge).
Blegen, Carl W. 1920. "Corinth in Prehistoric Times," *American Journal of Archaeology*, 24.1: 1–13.
Blomberg, Craig L. 1995. *1 Corinthians*, The NIV Application Commentary (Grand Rapids, MI: Zondervan Academic).

Bond, Helen. 2003. "Paul, the Corinthians, and Reconciliation," *Studies in World Christianity*, 9.2: 189–284.
Bookidis, Nancy. 2005. "Religion in Corinth: 146 B.C.E. to 100 C.E.," in *Urban Religion in Roman Corinth: Interdisciplinary Approaches*, ed. by Daniel Schowalter and Steven J. Friesen (Cambridge, MA: Harvard University Press), pp. 141–64.
Boswell, John. 2015. *Christianity, Social Tolerance, and Homosexuality: Gay People in Western Europe from the Beginning of the Christian Era to the Fourteenth Century* (Chicago, IL: University of Chicago Press).
Brown, Raymond E. 1997. *An Introduction to the New Testament*, The Anchor Yale Bible Reference Library (New Haven, CT: Yale University Press).
Budin, Stephanie L. 2008. *The Myth of Sacred Prostitution in Antiquity* (New York: Cambridge University Press).
Budin, Stephanie L. 2009. "Strabo's Hierodules: Corinth, Comana, and Eryx," in *Tempelprostitution im Altertum: Fakten unde Fiktionen*, ed. by Tanja S. Scheer and Martin Linfer (Berlin: Verlag-Antike), pp. 198–220.
Burk, Denny. 2008. "Discerning Corinthian Slogans through Paul's Use of the Diatribe in 1 Corinthians 6:12–20," *Bulletin for Biblical Research*, 18.1: 99–121.
Campbell, Douglas A. 2002. "Apostolic Competition at Corinth?," *Journal of Beliefs & Values*, 23.2: 229–31.
Castelli, Elizabeth A. 1991. *Imitating Paul: A Discourse of Power* (Louisville, KY: Westminster John Knox Press).
Collins, Adela Yarbro. 1980. "The Function of 'Excommunication' in Paul," *The Harvard Theological Review*, 73.1/2: 251–63.
Collins, Raymond F. 1999. *First Corinthians*, Sacra Pagina Series, 7, ed. by Daniel J. Harrington (Collegeville, MN: Liturgical Press).
Conzelmann, Hans. 1974. "Korinth Und Die Mädchen Der Aphrodite: Zur Religionsgeschichte Der Stadt Korinth," in *Theologie Als Schriftauslegung. Aufsätze Zum Neuen Testament*, Beiträge Zur Evangelischen Theologie, 65 (Munchen: Kaiser), pp. 152–66.
Conzelmann, Hans. 1975. *1 Corinthians*, Hermeneia: A Critical and Historical Commentary on the Bible (Philadelphia, PA: Fortress Press).
Cook III, William F. 2002. "Twenty-First Century Problems in a First Century Church (1 Corinthians 5–7)," *The Southern Baptist Journal of Theology*, 6.3: 44–57.
Dahl, Nils A. 1967. "Paul and the Church at Corinth in 1 Cor. 1:10–4:21," in *Christian History and Interpretation: Studies Presented to John Knox*, ed. by W. R. Farmer, C. F. D. Moule and R. R. Niebuhr (Cambridge: Cambridge University Press), pp. 313–35.
Deissmann, Adolf. 1957. *Paul: A Study in Social and Religious History*, Harper Torchbooks ; TB15 (New York: HarperOne).
DeMaris, Richard E. 1995. "Corinthian Religion and Baptism for the Dead (1 Corinthians 15:29): Insights from Archaeology and Anthropology." *Journal of Biblical Literature*, 114.4: 661–82.
Emmett, Grace. 2021. "The Apostle Paul's Maternal Masculinity," *Journal of Early Christian History*, 11.1: 15–37.
Engels, Donald. 1990. *Roman Corinth: An Alternative Model for the Classical City* (Chicago, IL: University of Chicago Press).

Enslin, Morton S. 1938. "'Luke' and Paul," *Journal of the American Oriental Society*, 58.1: 81–91.

Enslin, Morton S. 1970. "Once Again, Luke and Paul," 61.3–4: 253–71.

Fee, Gordon D. 1980. "Tongues—Least of the Gifts: Some Exegetical Observations on 1 Corinthians 12–14," *Pneuma*, 2.2: 3–14.

Fee, Gordon D. 1988. *The First Epistle to the Corinthians*, New International Commentary on the New Testament (Grand Rapids, MI: Eerdmans).

Fee, Gordon D. and Douglas Stuart. 1993. *How to Read the Bible for All Its Worth* (Grand Rapids, MI: Zondervan Academic).

Fellows, Richard G. 2022. "Early Sexist Textual Variants, and Claims That Prisca, Junia, and Julia Were Men," *The Catholic Biblical Quarterly*, 84.2: 252–78.

Fitzmyer, Joseph A. 2008. *First Corinthians: A New Translation with Introduction and Commentary*, The Anchor Yale Bible, 32 (New Haven, CT: Yale University Press).

Friesen, Steven J. 2004. "Poverty in Pauline Studies: Beyond the So-Called New Consensus," *Journal for the Study of the New Testament*, 26.3: 323–61.

Friesen, Steven J. 2010. "The Wrong Erastus: Ideology, Archaeology, and Exegesis," in *Corinth in Context: Comparative Studies on Religion and Society*, ed. by Steven J. Friesen, Dan Schowalter and James Walters (Leiden: Brill), pp. 231–56.

Gaca, Kathy L. 2003. *The Making of Fornication: Eros, Ethics, and Political Reform in Greek Philosophy and Early Christianity*, Hellenistic Culture and Society (Berkeley, CA: University of California Press), XL.

Gadamer, Hans-Georg. 1989. *Truth and Method*, 2nd rev. Edition ed. / trans. by Joel Weinsheimer and Donald G. Marshall. (New York: Crossroad).

Gaventa, Beverly R. 1996. "Our Mother St. Paul: Toward the Recovery of Neglected Theme," *The Princeton Seminary Bulletin*, XVII.1: 29–44.

Gaventa, Beverly R. 2017. "Mother's Milk and Ministry in 1 Corinthians 3," in *Theology and Ethics in Paul and His Interpreters: Essays in Honor of Victor Paul Furnish*, ed. by Eugene H. Lovering Jr and Jerry L. Sumney (Eugene, OR: Wipf and Stock), pp. 101–13.

Gilhuly, Kate. 2017. *Erotic Geographies in Ancient Greek Literature and Culture* (London: Routledge).

Glancy, Jennifer A. 2015. "The Sexual Use of Slaves: A Response to Kyle Harper on Jewish and Christian Porneia," *Journal of Biblical Literature*, 134.1: 215–29.

Gorman, Michael. 2017. *Apostle of the Crucified Lord* (Grand Rapids, MI: Eerdmans).

Goulder, Michael D. 1986. "Did Luke Know Any of the Pauline Letters?," *Perspectives in Religious Studies*, 13.2: 97–112.

Goulder, Michael D. 1991. "ΣΟΦΙΑ in 1 Corinthians," *New Testament Studies*, 37.4: 516–34.

Goulder, Michael D. 1999. "Libertines? (1 Cor. 5-6)," *Novum Testamentum*, 41.4: 334–48.

Harper, Kyle. 2012. "Porneia: The Making of a Christian Sexual Norm," *Journal of Biblical Literature*, 131.2: 363–83.

Harper, Kyle. 2013. *From Shame to Sin* (Cambridge, MA: Harvard University Press).

Harris, Gerald. 1991. "The Beginnings of Church Discipline: 1 Corinthians 5," *New Testament Studies*, 37.1: 1–21.

Hays, Richard B. 2011. *First Corinthians: Interpretation: A Bible Commentary for Teaching and Preaching*, Interpretation: A Bible Commentary for Teaching and Preaching (Louisville, KY: Westminster John Knox Press).

Hengel, Martin. 1977. *Crucifixion: In the Ancient World and the Folly of the Message of the Cross*, trans. by John Bowden (Philadelphia, PA: Fortress Press).

Hoke, Jimmy. 2021. *Feminism, Queerness, Affect, and Romans: Under God?*, Early Christianity and Its Literature, 30 (Atlanta, GA: SBL Press).

Horrell, David G. 2000. *The Social Ethos of the Corinthian Correspondence: Interests and Ideology from 1 Corinthians to 1 Clement*, Studies of the New Testament and Its World (Edinburgh: Bloomsbury T&T Clark).

Horrell, David G. 2009. "Aliens and Strangers? The Socioeconomic Location of the Addresses of 1 Peter," in *Engaging Economics: New Testament Scenarios and Early Christian Reception*, ed. by Bruce W. Longenecker and Kelly D. Liebengood (Grand Rapids, MI: Eerdmans), pp. 176–202.

Horsley, Richard A. 1977. "Wisdom of Word and Words of Wisdom in Corinth," *The Catholic Biblical Quarterly*, 39.2: 224–39.

Horsley, Richard A. 2011. *1 Corinthians*, Abingdon New Testament Commentaries (Nashville, TN: Abingdon Press).

Hurd, John Coolidge. 1983. *The Origin of I Corinthians* (Atlanta, GA: Mercer University Press).

Johanson, B. C. 1979. "Tongues, a Sign for Unbelievers?: A Structural and Exegetical Study of I Corinthians XIV. 20–25," *New Testament Studies*, 25.02: 180–203.

Johnson, Alan F. 2010. *1 Corinthians* (Downers Grove, IL: InterVarsity Press).

Johnson-debaufre, Melanie and Laura Nasrallah. 2011. "Beyond the Heroic Paul: Toward a Feminist and Decolonizing Approach to the Letters of Paul," in *The Colonized Apostle: Paul Through Postcolonial Eyes*, ed. by Christopher Stanley (Minneapolis., MN: Fortress Press), pp. 161–74.

Johnson, Jenna. 2023. "'A Lot of People Are Saying ... ': How Trump Spreads Conspiracies and Innuendoes," *Washington Post* https://www.washingtonpost.com/politics/a-lot-of-people-are-saying-how-trump-spreads-conspiracies-and-innuendo/2016/06/13/b21e59de-317e-11e6-8ff7-7b6c1998b7a0_story.html [accessed July 31, 2023].

Johnson, Luke Timothy. 1998. *Religious Experience in Earliest Christianity: A Missing Dimension in New Testament Study* (Minneapolis, MN: Fortress Press).

Johnston, Philip S. 2013. *The IVP Introduction to the Bible* (Downers Grove, IL: InterVarsity Press).

Keck, Leander E. 1979. *Paul and His Letters* (Philadelphia, PA: Fortress Press).

Kee, Howard Clark. 1997. *To Every Nation under Heaven: The Acts of the Apostles*, The New Testament in Context (Harrisburg, PA: Trinity Press International).

Keener, Craig S. 2005. *1–2 Corinthians*, The New Cambridge Bible Commentary (Cambridge: Cambridge University Press).

Kennedy, James H. 1897. "Are There Two Epistles in 2 Corinthians?," *The Expositor*, 6.3: 231–8.

Kistemaker, Simon J. 1992. "'Deliver This Man to Satan' (1 Cor. 5:5): A Case Study in Church Discipline," *Masters Seminary Journal*, 3.1: 33–45.

Klauck, Hans-Josef. 2006. *Ancient Letters and the New Testament: A Guide to Context and Exegesis* (Waco, TX: Baylor University Press).

Kloppenborg, John S. 2011. "Greco-Roman Thiasoi, the Ekklēsia at Corinth, and Conflict Management," in *Redescribing Paul and the Corinthians*, Early Christianity and Its Literature, 5, ed. by Ron Cameron and Merrill P. Miller (Atlanta, GA: Society of Biblical Literature), pp. 187–281.

Knox, John. 1966. "Acts and the Pauline Letter Corpus," in *Studies in Luke-Acts: Essays Presented in Honor of Paul Schubert, Buckingham Professor of New Testament Criticism and Interpretation at Yale University*, ed. by Leander E. Keck and James Louis Martyn (Nashville, TN: Abingdon Press), pp. 279–87.

Kurek-Chomycz, Dominika A. 2006. "Is There an 'Anti-Priscan' Tendency in the Manuscripts? Some Textual Problems with Prisca and Aquila," *Journal of Biblical Literature*, 125.1: 107–28.

Kwon, Oh-Young. 2010. "A Critical Review of Recent Scholarship on the Pauline Opposition and the Nature of Its Wisdom (Σοφία) in 1 Corinthians 1–4," *Currents in Biblical Research*, 8.3: 386–427.

Lassen, Eva Maria. 1991. "The Use of the Father Image in Imperial Propaganda and 1 Corinthians 4:14-21," *Tyndale Bulletin*, 42.1: 127–36.

Lin, Yii-Jan. 2024. "Of Escoffier, Gastronomie, Craft, and Canon," in *Reading in These Times*, 169th–188th Edition, ed. by Tat-Siong Benny Liew and Fernando F. Segovia (Atlanta, GA: SBL Press).

Lombaard, Christo. 2009. "Does Contextual Exegesis Require an Affirming Bible? Lessons from 'Apartheid' and 'Africa' as Narcissistic Hermeneutical Keys," *Scriptura: Journal for Biblical, Theological and Contextual Hermeneutics*, 101: 274–87.

Longenecker, Bruce W. 2009. "Exposing the Economic Middle: A Revised Economy Scale for the Study of Early Urban Christianity," *Journal for the Study of the New Testament*, 31.3: 243–78.

Longenecker, Bruce W. 2010. *Remember the Poor: Paul, Poverty, and the Greco-Roman World* (Grand Rapids, MI: Eerdmans).

Marchal, Joseph A. 2014. "Female Masculinity in Corinth?: Bodily Citations and the Drag of History," *Neotestamentica*, 48.1: 93–113.

Martin, Dale B. 1991. "Tongues of Angels and Other Status Indicators," *Journal of the American Academy of Religion*, 59.3: 547–89.

Martin, Dale B. 1999. *The Corinthian Body* (New Haven, CT: Yale University Press).

May, Alistair. 2004. *The Body for the Lord: Sex and Identity in 1 Corinthians 5–7*, Journal for the Study of the New Testament Supplement Series, 278 (London: Bloomsbury T&T Clark).

McNamara, Derek. 2010. "Shame the Incestuous Man: 1 Corinthians 5," *Neotestamentica*, 44.2: 307–26.

Meeks, Wayne A. 2003. *The First Urban Christians: The Social World of the Apostle Paul*, Second Edition (New Haven, CT: Yale University Press).

Meggitt, Justin. 2000. *Paul, Poverty and Survival*, Studies of the New Testament and Its World (Edinburgh: T&T Clark).

Millis, Benjamin W. 2010. "The Social and Ethnic Origins of the Colonists in Early Roman Corinth," in *Corinth in Context: Comparative Studies on Religion and Society*, ed. by Steven J. Friesen, Daniel N. Schowalter and James C. Walters (Leiden: Brill), pp. 13–35.

Mitchell, Margaret M. 1989. "Concerning Περὶ Δέ in 1 Corinthians," *Novum Testamentum*, 31.3: 229–56.

Mitchell, Margaret M. 1991. *Paul and the Rhetoric of Reconciliation: An Exegetical Investigation of the Language and Composition of 1 Corinthians* (Louisville, KY: Westminster John Knox Press).

Mitchell, Margaret M. 2003. "The Corinthian Correspondence and the Birth of Pauline Hermeneutics," in *Paul and the Corinthians: Studies on a Community in Conflict: Essays in Honour of of Margaret Thrall*, ed. by Trevor J. Burke and J. Keith Elliott, Supplements to Novum Testamentum (Leiden: Brill), pp. 17–53.

Moss, Candida R. 2023. "The Secretary: Enslaved Workers, Stenography, and the Production of Early Christian Literature," *The Journal of Theological Studies*, 74.1: 20–56.

Moss, Candida R. 2024. *God's Ghostwriters: Enslaved Christians and the Making of the Bible* (New York: Little, Brown and Company).

Muir, John. 2012. *Life and Letters in the Ancient Greek World* (London: Routledge).

Murphy-O'Connor, Jerome. 1978. "Corinthian Slogans in 1 Cor 6:12-20," *The Catholic Biblical Quarterly*, 40.3: 391–6.

Murphy-O'Connor, Jerome. 2002. *St. Paul's Corinth: Texts and Archaeology*, Third Revised and Expanded Edition (Collegeville, MN: Michael Glazier Book).

Myers, Alicia D. 2017. *Blessed among Women?: Mothers and Motherhood in the New Testament* (New York: Oxford University Press).

Myrou, Augustine. 1999. "Sosthenes: The Former Crispus(?)," *Greek Orthodox Theological Review*, 44.1–4: 207–12.

Naerebout, Frederick G. and Henk W. Singor. 2014. *Antiquity: Greeks and Romans in Context* (West Sussex and Malden, MA: Wiley-Blackwell).

Nasrallah, Laura Salah. 2014. "'You Were Bought with a Price': Freedpersons and Things in 1 Corinthians," in *Corinth in Contrast: Studies in Inqualiy*, ed. by Steven J. Friesen, Sarah A. James and Daniel N. Schowalter (Leiden: Brill), pp. 54–73.

Nasrallah, Laura Salah. 2021. "Judgment, Justice, and Destruction: Defixiones and 1 Corinthians," *Journal of Biblical Literature*, 140.2: 347–67.

Nasrallah, Laura Salah. 2024. *Ancient Christians and the Power of Curses: Magic, Aesthetics, and Justice* (Cambridge: Cambridge University Press).

"New York School Apologises for Reciting Pledge of Allegiance in Arabic," 2015. *The Guardian*, section US news http://www.theguardian.com/us-news/2015/mar/19/ny-school-apologises-reciting-pledge-of-allegiance-arabic [accessed April 27, 2016].

Økland, Jorunn. 2005. *Women in Their Place: Paul and the Corinthian Discourse of Gender and Sanctuary Space* (London: Bloomsbury T&T Clark).

Oyetade, Michael Oyebowale. 2020. "A Study of Speaking in Tongues in Acts and 1 Corinthians and Its Use and Abuse in Some Selected Contemporary Churches in Nigeria," *Stellenbosch Theological Journal*, 6.1: 477–98.

Pawlak, Marcin N. 2013. "Corinth after 44 BC: Ethnical and Cultural Changes," *Electrum*, 20: 143–62.

Penner, Todd. 2004. *In Praise of Christian Origins: Stephen and the Hellenists in Lukan Apologetic Historiography*, Emory Studies in Early Christianity (New York: T&T Clark).

Peterson, Dwight. 2021. *The Origins of Mark: The Markan Community in Current Debate* (Leiden: Brill).

Pettegrew, David K. 2016. "The Changing Rural Horizons of Corinth's First Urban Christians," in *The First Urban Churches 2: Roman Corinth*, ed. by James R. Harrison and L. L. Welborn (Atlanta, GA: SBL Press), pp. 153–83.

Poirier, John C. 2010. *The Tongues of Angels: The Concept of Angelic Languages in Classical Jewish and Christian Texts*, Wissenschaftliche Untersuchungen Zum Neuen Testament 2. Reihe, 287 (Tübingen: Mohr Siebeck).

Prior, David. 2020. *The Message of 1 Corinthians* (Downers Grove, IL: InterVarsity Press).

Reinhartz, Adele. 2002. *Befriending The Beloved Disciple: A Jewish Reading of the Gospel of John* (New York: Continuum).

Reinhartz, Adele. 2009. "Judaism in the Gospel of John," *Interpretation*, 63.4: 382–93.

Reno, Joshua M. 2016. "Γυνὴ Τοῦ Πατρός: Analytic Kin Circumlocution and the Case for Corinthian Adultery," *Journal of Biblical Literature*, 135.4: 827–47.

Reno, Joshua M. 2018. "Struggling Sages: Pauline Rhetoric and Social Control," *Catholic Biblical Quarterly*, 80.3: 491–511.

Reno, Joshua M. 2021. "Pornographic Desire in the Pauline Corpus," *Journal of Biblical Literature*, 140.1: 163–85.

Robinson, Betsey A. 2005. "Fountains and the Formation of Cultural Identity at Roman Corinth," in *Urban Religion in Roman Corinth: Interdisciplinary Approaches*, ed. by Daniel Schowalter and Steven J. Friesen (Cambridge, MA: Harvard Divinity School), pp. 101–40.

Robinson, Jonathan Rivett. 2018. "The Argument against Attributing Slogans in 1 Corinthians 6:12-20," *Journal for the Study of Paul and His Letters*, 8.1-2: 147–66.

Roebuck, Carl. 1972. "Some Aspects of Urbanization in Corinth," *Hesperia: The Journal of the American School of Classical Studies at Athens*, 41.1: 96–127.

Roebuck, Mary C. 1990. "Archaic Architectural Terracottas from Corinth," *Hesperia: The Journal of the American School of Classical Studies at Athens*, 59.1: 47–63.

Romano, David Gilman. 1994. "Post-146 B.C. Land Use in Corinth, and Planning of the Roman Colony of 44 B.C.," in *The Corinthia in the Roman Period: Including the Papers Given at a Symposium Held at the Ohio State University on 7–9 March, 1991*, Journal of Roman Archaeology Supplementary Series, 8, ed. by Timothy E. Gregory (Ann Arbor, MI: Journal of Roman Archaeology), pp. 9–30.

Romano, David Gilman. 2003. "City Planning, Centuriation, and Land Division in Roman Corinth: Colonia Laus Iulia Corinthiensis & Colonia Iulia Flavia Augusta Corinthiensis," in *Corinth, the Centenary, 1896–1996*, ed. by Charles K., Williams II and Nancy Bookidis (Princeton, NJ: American School of Classical Studies at Athens), pp. 280–301.

Romano, David Gilman. 2005. "A Roman Circus in Corinth," *Hesperia*, 74.4: 585–611.

Rosenfeld, Ben-Zion and Haim Perlmutter. 2011. "The Poor as a Stratum of Jewish Society in Roman Palestine 70–250 CE: An Analysis," *Historia: Zeitschrift Für Alte Geschichte*, 60.3: 273–300.

Rosner, Brian S. 1994. *Paul, Scripture and Ethics: A Study of 1 Corinthians 5–7*, Arbeiten Zur Geschichte Des Antiken Judentums Und Des Urchristentums, 22 (Leiden: Brill).

Rosner, Brian S. 1998. "Temple Prostitution in 1 Corinthians 6:12-20," *Novum Testamentum*, 40.4: 336–51.

Rutgers, Leonard Victor. 1994. "Roman Policy towards the Jews: Expulsions from the City of Rome during the First Century C.E.," *Classical Antiquity*, 13.1: 56–74.

Said, Edward W. 2003. *Orientalism* (New York: Penguin Books).

Sanders, Boykin. 2007. "1 Corinthians," in *True to Our Native Land: An African American New Testament Commentary*, ed. by Brian K. Blount, Cain Hope Felder, Clarice J. Martin and Emerson B. Powery (Minneapolis: Fortress Press), pp. 276–306.

Sanders, Guy D. R. 2005. "Urban Corinth: An Introduction," in *Urban Religion in Roman Corinth: Interdisciplinary Approaches*, ed. by Daniel Schowalter and Steven J. Friesen (Cambridge, MA: Harvard University Press), pp. 11–24.

Sayegh, Briggette. 2025. "Controversy over Pine Bush CSD Pledge of Allegiance Language," *TWC News* http://www.twcnews.com/nys/hudson-valley/news/2015/03/18/controversy-over-pine-bush-csd-pledge-of-allegiance-language.html [accessed April 27, 2016].

Schleiermacher, Friedrich. 1998. *Hermeneutics and Criticism*, trans. by Andrew Bowie (Cambridge: Cambridge University Press).

Schüssler Fiorenza, Elisabeth. 1989. "Text and Reality—Reality as Text: The Problem of a Feminist Historical and Social Reconstruction Based on Texts," *Studia Theologica—Nordic Journal of Theology*, 43.1: 19–34.

Schüssler Fiorenza, Elisabeth. 1994. *In Memory of Her: A Feminist Theological Reconstruction of Christian Origins* (New York: Crossroad).

Silverstein, Jason and Melissa Chan. 2015. "School Divided Over Reading Pledge of Allegiance in Arabic," *NY Daily News* http://www.nydailynews.com/news/national/school-divided-reading-pledge-allegiance-arabic-article-1.2154933 [accessed April 27, 2016].

Smith, David Raymond. 2009. *"Hand This Man over to Satan": Curse, Exclusion and Salvation in 1 Corinthians 5*, The Library of New Testament Studies (London: T&T Clark).

Smith, Jay E. 2008. "The Roots of a 'Libertine' Slogan in 1 Corinthians 6:18," *The Journal of Theological Studies*, 59.1: 63–95.

Smith, Mitzi J. 2023. *Chloe and Her People: A Womanist Critical Dialogue with First Corinthians* (Eugene, OR: Cascade Books).

Spawforth, Anthony J. S. 1996. "Roman Corinth: The Formation of a Colonial Elite," in *Roman Onomastics in the Greek East: Social and Political Aspects*, ΜΕΛΕΤΗΜΑΤΑ, 21, ed. by Athanasios D. Rizakis (Athens, GA, and Paris: Diffusion de Boccard), pp. 167–82.

Starnes, Todd. 2015. "One Nation under Allah: Fury after School Recites Pledge In Arabic," *Fox News* http://www.foxnews.com/opinion/2015/03/20/one-nation-under-allah-fury-after-school-recites-pledge-in-arabic.html [accessed April 27, 2016].

Stendahl, Krister. 1976. *Paul among Jews and Gentiles and Other Essays* (Philadelphia, PA: Fortress Press).

Sterling, Gregory E. 1992. *Historiography and Self-Definition: Josephos, Luke-Acts and Apologetic Historiography*, Supplements to Novum Testamentum (Leiden, Netherlands: Brill), LXIV.

Sterling, Gregory E. 2023. *Shaping the Past to Define the Present: Luke-Acts and Apologetic Historiography* (Grand Rapids, MI: Eerdmans).
Stowers, Stanley Kent. 1986. *Letter Writing in Greco-Roman Antiquity* (Philadelphia, PA: Westminster Press).
Theissen, Gerd. 2004. *The Social Setting of Pauline Christianity: Essays on Corinth* (Eugene, Oregon: Wipf & Stock Pub).
Thiong'o, Ngũgĩ wa. 1986. *Decolonising the Mind: The Politics of Language in African Literature* (New York: Boydell & Brewer).
Thiselton, Anthony C. 2013. *The First Epistle to the Corinthians*, The New International Greek Testament Commentary (Grand Rapids, MI: Eerdmans).
Tite, Philip L. 2010. "How To Begin, And Why? Diverse Functions of The Pauline Prescript Within a Greco-Roman Context," in *Paul and the Ancient Letter Form*, ed. by Stanley E. Porter and Sean A. Adams. Pauline Studies 6 (Leiden: Brill), pp. 57–99.
Tomlinson, Richard A. 1992. *From Mycenae to Constantinople: The Evolution of the Ancient City* (London and New York: Routledge).
Trebilco, Paul. 2011. *Self-Designations and Group Identity in the New Testament* (Cambridge: Cambridge University Press).
Tupamahu, Ekaputra. 2022. *Contesting Languages: Heteroglossia and the Politics of Language in the Early Church* (Oxford, New York: Oxford University Press).
"US Pledge of Allegiance in Arabic Leads School to Apologise," 2015. *BBC News* http://www.bbc.com/news/31989874 [accessed April 27, 2016].
Vielhauer, Phillip. 1975. "Paulus Und Die Kephaspartei in Korinth," *New Testament Studies*, 21.3: 341–52.
Vos, Craig Steven De. 1998. "Stepmothers, Concubines and the Case of Πορνεία in 1 Corinthians 5," *New Testament Studies*, 44.1: 104–14.
Walbank, Mary E. Hoskins. 1997. "The Foundation and Planning of Early Roman Corinth," *Journal of Roman Archaeology*, 10: 95–130.
Walker, Dawson. 1906. *The Gift of Tongues and Other Essays* (Edinburgh: T. & T. Clark).
Warner, Todd Huston. 2015. "NY High School Makes Kids Recite Pledge of Allegiance in Arabic Featuring 'One Nation Under Allah'," *Right Wing News* http://rightwingnews.com/democrats/ny-high-school-makes-kids-recite-pledge-of-allegiance-in-arabic-featuring-one-nation-under-allah/ [accessed April 27, 2016].
Watson, Francis. 1984. "2 Cor. X-Xiii and Paul's Painful Letter to the Corinthians," *The Journal of Theological Studies*, 35.2: 324–46.
Welborn, Larry L. 1987. "On the Discord in Corinth: 1 Corinthians 1–4 and Ancient Politics," *Journal of Biblical Literature*, 106.1: 85–111.
Welborn, L. L. 1995. "The Identification of 2 Corinthians 10-13 with the 'Letter of Tears'," *Novum Testamentum*, 37.2: 138–53.
Wenham, David. 1997. "Whatever Went Wrong in Corinth?," *The Expository Times*, 108.5: 137–41.
Wheeler-Reed, David, Jennifer W. Knust and Dale B. Martin. 2018. "Can a Man Commit Πορνεία with His Wife?," *Journal of Biblical Literature*, 137.2: 383–98.
Williams, Cyril G. 1975. "Glossolalia as a Religious Phenomenon: 'Tongues' at Corinth and Pentecost," *Religion*, 5.1: 16–32.
Wire, Antoinette Clark. 1990. *The Corinthian Women Prophets: A Reconstruction through Paul's Rhetoric* (Minneapolis, MN: Fortress Press).

Witherington III, Ben. 1995. *Conflict and Community in Corinth: A Socio-Rhetorical Commentary on 1 and 2 Corinthians* (Grand Rapids, MI: Eerdmans).

Yongnan, Jeon Ahn. 2013. *Interpretation of Tongues and Prophecy in 1 Corinthians 12–14, with a Pentecostal Hermeneutics*, Journal of the Pentecostal Theology Supplement Series, 41 (Blandford Forum: Deo Publishing).

Zaas, Peter S. 1984. "'Cast Out the Evil Man from Your Midst' (1 Cor 5:13b)," *Journal of Biblical Literature*, 103.2: 259–61.

INDEX OF AUTHORS

Adams, Sean A. 35, 38, 48
Ahmed, Sara 11

Bakhtin, M. M. 4
Barclay, John M. 51, 91
Barclay, William 1
Barrett, C. K. 1, 40, 43–4
Baur, F. C. 35, 40, 76, 78
Best, Ernest 77
Bhabha, Homi K. 93
Blegen, Carl W. 29
Blomberg, Craig L. 67
Bond, Helen 16
Bookidis, Nancy 31
Boswell, John 68
Brown, Raymond E. 17, 39
Budin, Stephanie L. 63–4
Burk, Denny 5

Campbell, Douglas A. 43
Castelli, Elizabeth A. 43, 57
Collins, Adela Yarbro 67
Collins, Raymond F. 14, 67
Conzelmann, Hans 67, 71, 81

Dahl, Nils A. 40–2
Deissmann, Adolf 37

Emmett, Grace 53, 55
Engels, Donald. 31
Enslin, Morton S. 38

Fee, Gordon D. 3, 14–15, 20, 39, 45, 67, 81
Fellows, Richard G. 36
Fitzmyer, Joseph A. 14, 66
Friesen, Steven J. 39, 50–2, 82

Gaca, Kathy L. 71
Gadamer, Hans-Georg 3
Gaventa, Beverly R. 44, 54
Gilhuly, Kate 64
Glancy, Jennifer A. 69
Gorman, Michael 1
Goulder, Michael D. 5, 38, 40, 67

Harper, Kyle 69
Harris, Gerald 67
Hays, Richard B. 42, 48, 85
Hengel, Martin 48
Hoke, Jimmy 69
Horrell, David G. 16, 51, 70
Horsley, Richard A. 39–40
Hurd, John Coolidge 18

Johanson, B. C. 82
Johnson, Alan F. 1
Johnson, Jenna 66
Johnson-DeBaufre, Melanie 8
Johnson, Luke Timothy 77
Johnston, Philip S. 1

Keck, Leander E. 1
Kee, Howard Clark 35
Keener, Craig S. 71, 77
Kennedy, James H. 17
Kistemaker, Simon J. 67
Klauck, Hans-Josef 13
Kloppenborg, John S. 40
Knox, John 38
Kurek-Chomycz, Dominika A. 36
Kwon, Oh-Young 40

Lassen, Eva Maria. 55
Lin, Yii-Jan 2

Lombaard, Christo 2
Longenecker, Bruce W. 51

Marchal, Joseph A. 58
Martin, Dale B. 82
May, Alistair 67
McNamara, Derek 67
Meeks, Wayne A. 39, 50
Meggitt, Justin 52
Millis, Benjamin W. 31–2
Mitchell, Margaret M. 15–16, 18–19, 47
Moss, Candida R. 13–15
Muir, John 15
Murphy-O'Connor, Jerome. 5, 62–3
Myers, Alicia D. 55
Myrou, Augustine 38

Naerebout, Frederick G. 29
Nasrallah, Laura Salah 39, 42, 70

Økland, Jorunn 86
Oyetade, Michael Oyebowale 77

Pawlak, Marcin N. 31, 76
Penner, Todd 35
Peterson, Dwight 1
Pettegrew, David K. 30
Poirier, John C. 82
Prior, David 1

Reinhartz, Adele 8–9
Reno, Joshua M. 65–7
Robinson, Betsey A. 31
Robinson, Jonathan Rivett 5–6
Roebuck, Carl 29
Roebuck, Mary C. 29
Romano, David Gilman 30–1

Rosenfeld, Ben-Zion 51
Rosner, Brian S. 67
Rutgers, Leonard Victor 36

Said, Edward W. 6–7
Sanders, Boykin 51–2
Sanders, G.D.R. 30
Sayegh, Briggette 75
Schleiermacher, Friedrich 3
Smith, David Raymond 70
Smith, Jay E. 5
Smith, Mitzi J. 7, 39
Spawforth, Anthony J. S. 31
Starnes, Todd 75
Stendahl, Krister 77
Sterling, Gregory E. 35
Stowers, Stanley Kent 14–15

Theissen, Gerd 39, 50, 52
Thiselton, Anthony C. 39, 49, 79, 91
Trebilco, Paul 24

Vielhauer, Phillip 40
Vos, Craig Steven De 67

Walbank, Mary E. 31
Walker, Dawson 77
Watson, Francis 17
Welborn, L. L. 17, 39, 42
Wenham, David 1
Wheeler-Reed, David 68–9
Williams, Cyril G. 77
Wire, Antoinette Clark 2–3, 39

Yongnan, Jeon Ahn 77

Zaas, Peter S. 67

INDEX OF SUBJECTS

Acts 10, 14, 16, 24, 35–9, 41, 69, 77, 91
ancient letter 13
Apollos 10, 17, 29, 37–44, 47, 54, 56, 65
apostle 7, 14, 15, 20, 26, 72, 81–2, 92
   apostleship 15, 19, 26, 41
   super-apostles 17
authorial intention 2–4
authority 6–7, 10–11, 15–17, 20–1, 24–7, 36–8, 40–5, 47–9, 53, 55–60, 63–4, 72–3, 79–81, 90, 92–3

baptism 10, 26, 28, 42–3
benevolent patriarchalism 1
body 5, 19, 25, 28, 65, 71–2, 77–8, 81, 99
   body of Christ 27
   social body 81

Cephas 10, 40, 42–4, 47, 56
Chloe 16, 39, 51
   Chloe's people 10, 16, 18–20, 24, 39–40, 45, 65
Chrysostom 38, 67
class 30–1, 33, 37, 50, 59
collection 20, 28, 91–3
conflict 3–4, 17, 21, 37, 43, 48–50, 59, 87, 93
Corinthian slogans 4–6, 42
cross 10, 19, 24, 27–8, 43, 48–50, 52–3, 59
   crucifixion 48

divisions 8, 10, 16–17, 19, 24, 27, 33, 39–43, 45, 47, 54, 59, 93
   factionalism 10, 40, 43, 47, 54, 60

exegesis 3–4

faith 2, 6, 28, 34, 42, 52, 81, 83, 93
freedom 5–6, 25–6, 60

gender 27, 50, 54, 87
gospel 8, 10, 26–8, 41, 43, 45, 47–8, 53, 55, 59
   gospelizing 43, 47

hermeneutics 2–3
   biblical interpretation 2

identity 10, 20–1, 25, 29, 30–6, 44, 47–9, 52–3, 59, 73, 76, 86–7, 92–3

leadership 7, 10–11, 17, 21, 24, 41–5, 47–8, 56–9, 72, 90, 92–3

money 28, 62, 90–1

paulinist 35
Pentecostal/Charismatic 77
porneia 1, 4–5, 19, 25, 69, 97
   fornication 5, 68–9
   prostitute 30, 63–4, 68–9
   sexual immorality 8, 11, 16, 24–5, 64, 68–9
poverty 50–1
preaching 10, 27, 37, 43

resurrection 1, 10, 20, 27–8
rhetoric 3, 10, 52–3, 59, 61–2, 64–5, 70, 73, 82–3, 90

Sosthenes 14–15, 37–8

tongues 27, 76, 82–4, 86–7

foreign languages 11, 27
foreign tongues 85
glossolalia 77–8, 82
speaking in tongues 77, 84–5
Donald Trump 61–2, 64, 66, 69, 73

unity 10–11, 17, 44–5, 47, 49, 56, 59–60, 71, 73, 81, 84, 92–3

wisdom 24, 41, 44, 50, 52–3, 55–6, 81